A MESSAGE
WORTH
DYING
FOR

SIBERIAN MISSION

MIKE *and* DIANE
MEAGHER

A Message Worth Dying For

by Mike and Diane Meagher*
with Raymond L. Balogh, Jr

A Message Worth Dying For is also available on Amazon Kindle, Barnes & Noble Nook and Apple iBooks.

* "MEAGHER" is an ancient Gaelic/Irish name. In the branch of the clan I was raised in the name was enunciated: "MARR". Thanks for honoring the pronunciation!

13 Sept. '15

Pastor Jason and Ashley,

Walk in bold and humble obedience with a father's heart — basking in His love, power and grace!

Dr. Michael
& Diane

we2cold@ymail.com

1 Peter 4:2

"I didn't go to religion to make me happy. I always knew a bottle of Port would do that.

If you want a religion to make you feel really comfortable, I certainly don't recommend Christianity."

—C. S. LEWIS

"The safest place on this planet is in the center of God's will."

—MIKE MEAGHER

...for the accuser of our brethren has been thrown down, he who accuses them before our God day and night. "And they overcame him because of the blood of the Lamb and because of the word of their testimony, and they did not love their life even when faced with death.

—REV. 12:10B-11

CONTENTS

PART III: BIBLICAL REFLECTIONS

Part IV: Appendix

Mid-afternoon, November 1, 1999, north central Siberia ...

S HE NEVER SAW ME COMING.

That was understandable, as it was the onset of winter in Siberia, when thick habitation fog limits visibility to less than 10 feet, and the dusky midday sun barely skims the horizon.

Nor did she hear me approach. My handmade moose hide boots padded silently toward the frozen lake, and any rustling my thick fur-lined canvas coat made was drowned out by the fragile elderly widow's groans and sobs as she futilely tried to chop a watering hole in the thick ice with a heavy six-foot iron spike.

She was alone—except for relentless fear that a spirit of death would appear at any time to snuff out her life. She and her husband had crossed the shamans, whose reprisals were swift and lethal. They cursed her husband; a short time later, he died a mysterious, agonizing death. Even as she mourned the loss of her beloved, one of the shamans told her she was next ...

She looked up and there I stood: salt-and-peppered full beard and long hair matching my large badger fur hat, strangely complexioned, dressed in black, and head and shoulders taller than any man she had ever known.

I was scowling. Not at her, specifically, but at the depressing experiences I had had that day at the pedagogical college where I taught. During my two-mile walk back home, I was ruminating—with a good measure of self-pity—about the travails of being a pioneer missionary struggling to communicate the Gospel in Siberia's "Black Hole" region. My face simply mirrored the dark turmoil of my mind and heart.

But to her I was a portent of death. Her face reflected a horror I had never before seen in a human being, and she stood stock-still, with no strength to fight, flee, or even scream.

Though we had no language in common, we were both about to receive the customized whispers of love and mercy from a Father who knew exactly what each of His children needed at that moment.

Responding to His unmistakable nudge more out of stern duty than gentle compassion, I snatched the iron spike from the woman and attacked the ice in a silent rage that fueled the adrenaline needed to complete my unwelcomed task.

During my stubborn, persistent efforts, both of us began to change. The woman's expression migrated from terror, to puzzlement, to the unbridled delight of a little girl receiving a precious gift. Through my expenditure of energy, God melted my anger and frustration and replaced it with a growing softness of heart for this poor helpless woman.

Weariness set in and the excruciating cramping in my aging joints and hands mercifully turned to a blessed numbness from the -40° F cold. I started feeling an unwelcome lubrication beginning to weaken my grip when I was jolted by the woman's shriek. Wide eyed, she pointed to my gloves and the spike. Early frostbite and the vicious pounding were lacerating my hands and popping blisters. Blood seeped through my gloves and dripped languidly down the shaft.

As I saw my blood, the Holy Spirit kindled an indescribable love within my heart, and I looked at the woman again, this time with a warm, loving compassion that radiated from my frozen face and glazed eyes.

Finally, the spike broke through the thick ice. I lowered her small rope-suspended bucket into the hole and drew water for her and her animals. I handed her the bucket and the spike and we parted, both of us profoundly changed by the wordless encounter.

Ten minutes later, I was home, and for the next six hours, I sat alone in our cabin, nursing and praying over my wounds and meditating on the experience. That evening, Diane and our Sakha family returned, excitedly out-chattering each other to tell me of the "odd tale" that had just spread throughout several nearby villages:

A prominent widow told of how she was visited by an unknown spirit who had taken on flesh and bled in his hands to provide her with life-giving water ...

FOREWORD

THIS BOOK IS A GIFT to those special people our Father gave to us to make our lives and ministry together possible since 1975.

Except for a few place names, and pseudo names we will not use the actual names of individuals, organizations, or churches that have done us and our work good or evil. Each of you knows who you are. Our Father has promised that He alone will, on a day He has determined, bring full reward for good and evil. (2 Corinthians 5:9–10[1]; Revelation 22:12[2]).

There are so many who made our lives of service to Christ, and thus this book, possible. We would not steal your reward by exalting you before men in this life, but we'll be the first to applaud as our Savior says to you from His Bema seat, "Well done, good and faithful servant." Please know that you also have our deepest and sincerest gratitude for working alongside us and supporting us. We will

---

1. *Therefore we make it our aim, whether present or absent, to be well pleasing to Him. For we must all appear before the judgment seat of Christ, that each one may receive the things done in the body, according to what he has done, whether good or bad.*

2. *"And behold, I am coming quickly, and My reward is with Me, to give to every one according to his work."*

also not name those who, in reproaching and opposing our work, shamed themselves, us, Father, or His name and work. We will instead leave you to your task of personal reflection and repentance.

Invariably, wherever we have gone in nearly 40 years of marriage and ministry, people ask us, *"Why? Why do you insist on always taking on the tough, nasty, perilous, impossible assignments with no visible protection, advance provision, safety nets, or plans (let alone backup plans)? How can you be so stupid and presumptuous?"*

We respond: "We have learned through our many adventures that there is a fine line between bravery and stupidity, as well as between faith and presumption. That fine line is the voice of God. To obey His voice is bravery and faith; to disobey Him is stupidity and presumption. To be able to hear His voice requires true repentance and new birth, for Jesus said, *'My sheep hear my voice, I know them, and they follow me.'"* (John 10:27)

We fully understand that to most of our families, friends, and acquaintances, our life and lifestyle have always been strange—and actually offensive to many. This book seeks to explain our lives and internal compasses through our testimonies and a series of short vignettes.

Two simple fundamental truths underlie this book:

The Gospel of Jesus Christ is of infinite value and is truly to us a message worth living all out for—and

It is *"A Message Worth Dying For"*—dying daily to self and this world to be most effective in the building of His Kingdom.

D. L. Moody once said, "If we are full of pride and conceit and ambition and self-seeking and pleasure and the world, there is no room for the Spirit of God, and I believe many a man is praying to God to fill him when he is full already with something else."

Demonic, human, and worldly wisdoms do not comprehend what Diane and I are doing for our LORD or why we do it. But from a biblical perspective it makes perfect sense, *if* four things are true:

The Gospel of Jesus Christ is of ultimate value, not only for personal application, but also to live for and disseminate. (2 Timothy 2:3–4)[3]

The Kingdom of God is worth pursuing first at all cost. (Luke 12:22–31)[4]

Without faith (trust without safety nets) it is impossible to please God. (2 Chronicles 16:9a[5]; Hebrews 11:6)[6]

There is only one purpose for our lives: to obey the will of Him who put us here. (Isaiah 61:1–3)[7]

---

3. *You therefore must endure hardship as a good soldier of Jesus Christ. No one engaged in warfare entangles himself with the affairs of this life, that he may please him who enlisted him as a soldier.*

4. *Then He said to His disciples, "Therefore I say to you, do not worry about your life, what you will eat; nor about the body, what you will put on. Life is more than food, and the body is more than clothing. Consider the ravens, for they neither sow nor reap, which have neither storehouse nor barn; and God feeds them. Of how much more value are you than the birds? And which of you by worrying can add one cubit to his stature? If you then are not able to do the least, why are you anxious for the rest? Consider the lilies, how they grow: they neither toil nor spin; and yet I say to you, even Solomon in all his glory was not arrayed like one of these. If then God so clothes the grass, which today is in the field and tomorrow is thrown into the oven, how much more will He clothe you, O you of little faith? And do not seek what you should eat or what you should drink, nor have an anxious mind. For all these things the nations of the world seek after, and your Father knows that you need these things. But seek the Kingdom of God, and all these things shall be added to you.*

5. *For the eyes of the Lord run to and fro throughout the whole earth, to show Himself strong on behalf of those whose heart is loyal to Him.*

6. *But without faith it is impossible to please Him, for he who comes to God must believe that He is, and that He is a rewarder of those who diligently seek Him.*

7. *"The Spirit of the Lord God is upon Me,*
Because the Lord has anointed Me
To preach good tidings to the poor;
He has sent Me to heal the brokenhearted,
To proclaim liberty to the captives,
And the opening of the prison to those who are bound;
To proclaim the acceptable year of the Lord,
And the day of vengeance of our God;

We are exhorted: *Do not love the world or anything in the world. If anyone loves the world, the love of the Father is not in him. For everything in the world—the cravings of sinful man, the lust of his eyes and the boasting of what he has and does—comes not from the Father but from the world. The world and its desires pass away, but the man who does the will of God lives forever.* —1 John 2:15–17

So, starting in June, 1975, Diane and I determined together to lay aside whatever this world offered us in comforts, possessions, and distractions for the sake of following our Savior wherever, and to whomever, He would allow us to someday bring His love; to an unreached people of His choosing. In His sovereign love, He chose the final remnants of the ancient Medo-Persian Empire living today in north-central Siberia.

We received additional encouragement from the recorded thoughts of two inspirational men.

* * * * * *

Surrounding President John F. Kennedy's tomb in Arlington are large marble stones engraved with some of his quotes. Our favorite is from his January 20, 1961 inaugural speech:

"Let every nation know, whether it wishes us well or ill, that we shall pay any price, bear any burden, meet any hardship, support any friend, oppose any foe, to assure the survival and the success of liberty."

Diane and I long ago adapted this quote to reflect our firm commitment to lives sold out in the service and glory of God:

"Let everyone know, whether they wish us well or ill, that we, Michael and Diane Meagher, shall pay any price, bear any burden, meet any hardship, support any friend, oppose any foe, to assure the

---

To comfort all who mourn,
To console those who mourn in Zion,
To give them beauty for ashes,
The oil of joy for mourning,
The garment of praise for the spirit of heaviness;
That they may be called trees of righteousness,
The planting of the Lord, that He may be glorified."

*survival and the success of the Gospel of Jesus Christ through our
lives in our generation."*

* * * * * *

The late Rev. Dr. Alan Redpath, a beloved British evangelist and
pastor, authored seven books that ignited in me (Michael) a deep
passion to walk by faith[8]. From these treasured volumes, three
statements profoundly fortified our resolve during 21 years of difficult preparation:

*"Circumstances which we have resented, situations which we have
found desperately difficult, have all been the means in the hands of
God of driving the nails into the self-life which so easily complains."*

*"There's some task which the God of all the universe, the great
Creator, your redeemer in Jesus Christ has for you to do, and which
will remain undone and incomplete until by faith and obedience
you step into the will of God."*

*"When God wants to do an impossible task He takes an impossi-
ble man and crushes him."*

* * * * * *

To prepare us for the day He would lead us to an unreached people group, Father used us for the most part in places and situations
where we ministered alone and without fanfare. Yet we always knew
we were never truly alone or "Lone Rangers" in those efforts. Whenever we were called to step out in faith to do something perilous
or deemed impossible, Father always gifted us with a small team of
warriors who stood faithfully with us and surrounded us and our
work with prayer and provision.

To Him, and to them, we are eternally grateful.

---

8. *Victorious Christian Living* (1955), *Victorious Prayer* (1956), *Victorious
Christian Service* (1958), *The Royal Route to Heaven* (1960), *The Making of a
Man of God* (1962), *Blessings Out of Buffetings* (1965), *Law and Liberty* and
Captivity to Conquest (1978).

Part I:
Cast of Characters

CHAPTER 1

A Brief History of the Sakha People

THE LOVELY AND PRECIOUS TRIBAL peoples of the Sakha Republic share a long and storied history. The Sakha—or Yakut—a people formed from the mixture of local tribes, migrated to Siberia from the Turkic south about 1,200 years ago. Some of their number continued across the then existing land bridge spanning the Bering Straits and settled in North America, becoming some of the continent's original inhabitants. Unearthed artifacts confirm their travel as far south as the Los Angeles basin and eastward to North Carolina.

Yakutsk, the capital of The Sakha Republic (or Yakutia) was founded in 1632, and in 1922 the region was incorporated as an autonomous soviet socialist republic. In 1992, after the fall of the Soviet Union, Yakutia was recognized in Moscow as the largest of the ten autonomous Turkic republics under the jurisdiction of the Russian Federation.

The Sakha Republic is immense. At 1.2 million square miles, it comprises one fortieth of the Earth's land surface; 40 percent of the republic lies north of the Arctic Circle. The region boasts more than half a million rivers and about 800,000 lakes, nearly one for each of its residents (2010 population: 958,528).

Although more than one out of four Yakuts live in the capital city of Yakutsk (2010 population: 269,601), life is largely parochial. Of the remaining 496 towns in the Sakha Republic, only 33 sport populations of 5,000 or more.

Perhaps the most discussed feature of Yakutia is its extreme climate. Acknowledged as the coldest inhabited place on earth, temperatures routinely dip to -50° F—and for short periods to -70° F—during the seven-month winters. July's average temperature is 96° F, with summer temperatures of over 100° F being fairly common.

Though two-mile-deep permafrost underlies the entire republic (in fact, Yakutsk is the world's largest city built on continuous permafrost), many of the wealthier Sakha heat their homes with the area's abundant natural gas. They can't risk staying too warm, though, rarely heating their residences above 50° F to minimize the physical shock of stepping outside into the potentially lethal temperatures.

The Sakha Republic is rich in minerals and other underground treasures: oil, gas, coal, gold, silver, tin, and tungsten, among others. The republic produces over 25 percent of the diamonds mined in the world. Though the land is rich in such commodities, very little of the profit filters down to the Sakha people, most of whom lead spare and simple lives.

The short growing season still allows for a robust production of wheat, oats, potatoes, and cabbage. Cucumbers and tomatoes are largely grown under glass. Livestock includes pigs, horses, cows, chickens, and—in the northern regions—reindeer. Hunting and fishing are prevalent in the summer and fall, and many families subsist during the winter on the harvests of the skilled outdoorsmen who populate the republic. Fur trading is another staple of the economy.

In notable juxtaposition to American life, the Sakha raise horses for meat and dogs for fur. Frozen cubes of raw horse meat are a treat, much preferred by many children over ice cream as a dessert.

The Sakha people have been historically maltreated, maligned, and ignored by the remainder of the Russian populace. During the dawn of the nuclear age, Yakutia was chosen as a primary testing ground for detonating experimental weapons of mass destruction, and the resultant contamination persists to this day within every bite of locally grown food and every drink of river water.

For centuries, the region has been under the spiritual stranglehold of demonic forces, mediated through the shamans (witchdoctors) who hold the power of life, torment, and death over those who acquiesce to their power. Local Mafia-type syndicates also hold tremendous sway, and the Russian government exerts its ironfisted influence from afar.

Given their heritage of oppression, the Sakha people nevertheless remain a community of strong, hardworking, humble souls who value family and graciously extend hospitality toward humble and innocuous strangers, though they intractably reject the presence of condescending, threatening, and "holier than thou" visitors. They are a people of good humor, and enjoy long conversations punctuated with jokes, gags, and laughter. Though some among them are intensely distrustful of strangers, once they know one will respect them, and will be solid lifelong friends.

Such is the glorious harvest field for two ordinary Christian soldiers following their General's call to promote the Kingdom of God in remote north central Siberia.

CHAPTER 2

Mike's Testimony

We ought also to lay down our lives for the brethren.
—1 John 3:16

IT WAS, QUITE LITERALLY, "a dark and stormy night" in the waning hours of 1951 when the accident occurred. Richard K. Gershman—journalist, public relations representative for CBS, and son of Chicago Daily News magnate Isaac Gershman—was nervously negotiating a dark, slick highway during a road trip near Atlanta, when the creature appeared. With far too little warning for either accident victim to stop or veer to avoid a collision, Richard could only hold on and hope he wouldn't suffer too badly. Richard escaped without serious injury, but the deer crumpled, dead, in front of the car.

Seeking solace from the trauma of the accident, Richard turned to the arms of his lovely Jewish girlfriend, Irene. As a result of their intimate coupling that night, Richard left Irene with a precious gift—and then walked out of her life and never came back.

It was the third out-of-wedlock pregnancy for the 22-year-old Irene, but unlike the other two times, she chose to keep this baby. She would, however, need help ...

Shortly thereafter, she charmed a 26-year-old Pacific Theater WWII veteran, Georgia Tech grad, and Navy officer, Lt. Vincent Meagher. He had no reason to doubt Irene's declaration that the new life in her womb was his. So he committed to honor her—and his responsibilities—and shortly thereafter they wed. Stationed at the Pentagon and residing in Fairfax County, Virginia, Dad drove to the Bethesda Naval Hospital for my birth on September 28, 1952.

For the next 38 years, Mom and her sisters successfully kept their secret from Vince and from the world.

Among the great gifts my Heavenly Father gave me in life was to call Vince Meagher "Dad." Even though our relationship was often volatile, he poured so much—including himself—into my life in the all-too-brief 16 years I lived under his roof. Sadly, it took decades for me to truly appreciate him before (in 1996) he entered eternity.

From 1954 to 1964, two more boys and three girls were added to our family. We endured seven address changes in four states as Dad transferred from the Navy to aerospace engineering support for the early U.S. space program, for which Dad moved to Maitland, Florida in 1962. Six years later, I left for the minor Roman Catholic seminary near Philadelphia.

Dad was raised in a strict Irish Catholic home and was educated, from 1938 to 1941, at a high school military academy run by the Order of Mary (Marist Fathers) in Atlanta. He determined to raise his children with the deepest respect for, and fullest compliance with, the pre-Vatican II rites and rituals of his childhood faith, and he began in earnest with me.

During my early elementary years, people asked me what I wanted to be. I responded with confidence, "I'm going to be God!" I'm sure my parents received curious looks, as that position was eternally taken. One Sunday at mass I pointed to the officiating celebrant and exclaimed, "Look, God is holding up that pretty cup again!" With a sigh of relief, my parents taught me a new word which would embody my singular life goal: *"Priest."*

Dad was thrilled when, in early 1968, I asked him to help me to find a school where I could begin my studies for the priesthood. To have an eldest son enter into Holy Orders was a special honor to a Catholic dad. He conducted some enthusiastic research and soon located several of the Marist priests he had studied under at the Marist Military Academy in Atlanta 27 years earlier.

Three of his former teachers were on the faculty of Marist Preparatory School, an all-boys commuter and resident minor seminary in Langhorne, Pennsylvania, just north of Philadelphia. I entered Marist Prep as a sophomore in September, 1968, certain that I would discover or acquire the power and resolve to find peace with the God who had died on a cross for me.

Every day I participated in religious studies, three sets of community and private rosaries, mass with communion, confession, meditations, and not a few sacramental oblations. Still, even with all my prayers, works of charity, penance, and sacraments, I found neither peace with God nor the power to resist temptation. Actually, I experienced just the opposite. I found within me a growing lust for the world and all its offerings—those pleasures I would miss out on as a priest.

I didn't read the Bible in private, but I was haunted by a verse read in mass one morning, a verse whose implications I could not ignore: *"And because iniquity hath abounded, the love [for God] of many shall grow cold."*⁹ I reluctantly realized that the iniquity abounding in my heart (the love for my flesh's appetites) did not tolerate—indeed, actually chilled—my desire to love God. And none of the religious training or practice I had wholeheartedly and sincerely thrown myself into was going to change it.

As Easter Break 1969 approached, a "voice"—which I later understood to be the relentless beckoning of the Holy Spirit—began to haunt me with words I did not want to hear. Like an unwanted song playing over and over, the voice pursued me incessantly,

---

9. Matthew 24:12.

insistently: *"You have a religion, I want a relationship."* But I was never taught that there was a difference.

A few weeks after the voice started, I decided to spend Easter with my family a thousand miles south in Maitland, Florida.

But the Holy Spirit had already been there, arranging a divine appointment for me. A few months prior to my visit, a friend and neighbor of mine, who was also a Roman Catholic, surrendered to God in a dramatic encounter and emerged from that engagement an entirely different soul. The man I had known was peculiarly hard and vicious in word and action. The one I interacted with this time was a very different person who bubbled over with a joy and peace I did not have and could not conjure. I had never witnessed such a genuine transformation.

When I asked the source of his change, he recounted his surrender, and then asked with puzzlement, "Mike, don't you know Jesus?" Friend or not, his question deeply offended my religious pride, and I would have slugged him—if he hadn't been an NCAA football star, heavy-weight wrestler, bar bouncer ... and roughly twice my size. Didn't he know how dedicated I was to "the faith," studying to be a priest in the one true Church? As if in spiritual stereo, the Voice spoke again, *"You have a religion, I want a relationship."* My friend then read to me the following three passages from his (offensive version)[10] King James Bible:

For Christ is not entered into the holy places made with hands, which are the figures of the true, but into heaven itself, now to appear in the presence of God for us; Nor yet that He should offer Himself often, as the high priest entereth into the holy place every year with blood of others; For then must he often have suffered since the foundation of the world. But now once, in the end of the

---

10. From 1885 through the 1960s the Baltimore Catechism, the standard for American Roman Catholic faith and practice, declared the King James Version "anathema" ("accursed"). The only books authorized during that time to be consulted for religious purposes were those stamped on the first page inside the book's front cover with two official Church seals: *Imprimatur* ("let it be printed") and *Nihil Obstat* ("nothing objectionable").

ages {world} hath He appeared to put away sin by the sacrifice of Himself. And as it is appointed unto men once to die, but after this the judgment, So Christ was once offered to bear the sins of many; and unto them that look for Him shall He appear the second time without sin unto salvation. —Hebrews 9:24–28

Therefore being justified by faith, we have peace with God through our Lord Jesus Christ: By whom also we have access by faith into this grace wherein we stand, and rejoice in hope of the glory of God. And not only so, but we glory in tribulations also: knowing that tribulation worketh patience; And patience, experience; and experience, hope: And hope maketh not ashamed; because the love of God is shed abroad in our hearts by the Holy Ghost which is given unto us. For when we were yet without strength, in due time Christ died for the ungodly. For scarcely for a righteous man will one die: yet peradventure for a good man some would even dare to die. But God commendeth his love toward us, in that, while we were yet sinners, Christ died for us. Much more then, being now justified by his blood, we shall be saved from wrath through him. For if, when we were enemies, we were reconciled to God by the death of his Son, much more, being reconciled, we shall be saved by his life. And not only so, but we also joy in God through our Lord Jesus Christ, by whom we have now received the atonement. —Romans 5:1–11

If we receive the witness of men, the witness of God is greater: for this is the witness of God which he hath testified of his Son. He that believeth on the Son of God hath the witness in himself: he that believeth not God hath made him a liar; because he believeth not the record that God gave of his Son. And this is the record, that God hath given to us eternal life, and this life is in his Son. He that hath the Son hath life; and he that hath not the Son of God hath not life. These things have I written unto you that believe on the name of the Son of God; that ye may know that ye have eternal life, and that ye may believe on the name of the Son of God. And this is the confidence that we have in him, that, if we ask any thing according to his will, he heareth us: And if we know that he hear us, whatsoever

we ask, we know that we have the petitions that we desired of him.
—1 John 5:9–14

In those scriptures, God opened my understanding of a *relationship* with Him. I saw that in reality I had a relationship with a set of rules and regulations, a religious calendar, and ideas and stories about God—all without *knowing Him personally.* In God's economy, there was no room in my heart and life for religion *and* relationship; I had to choose one or the other. At my friend's leading, I knelt with him and repented of my sin, and asked for—and surrendered to—His FREE gift of eternal life. In return, God filled me with a previously unknown peace, release from guilt, and a sense of His presence that strengthened me during the next two years of deep theological, emotional, and spiritual conflicts.

I returned to the minor seminary, armed with a King James Version Bible and a quiver of questions. All "hell" broke loose as God's Spirit challenged my childhood faith and I challenged my Marist teachers. Looking back, I am so thankful that my Father confessor and spiritual advisor was a kind man who was also searching.

I began daily listening to Christian teaching on AM radio in Philadelphia. Gradually, steadily, my faith and practice grew from obeying Catholic dogmas to following Evangelical biblical directives. Over the next four years, I bought or borrowed every book and audio series available from Dr. James Boice, Dr. John R. Rice, Dr. Alan Redpath, "Back to the Bible," Dr. Lehman Strauss, the Moody Bible Series, Dr. Adrian Rogers, and others. I could not absorb enough of the Word and the tools to grasp it. I also read many biographies. God used the stories of David Brainerd, John Stam, Jim Elliott, and a young martyr in the Soviet Army named Vanya to inspire me to a life sold out to evangelism and missions.

In July 1971, as God was leading me from the Catholic Church, I "won the national lottery" (translation: I was drafted to serve in Vietnam). Wanting some say over the destiny of my young years, I immediately followed in my Dad's footsteps and joined the Navy. During my years in the Navy, Coast Guard, and with the National

Oceanic and Atmospheric Administration (NOAA), I had the honor of leading dozens of shipmates and others to saving faith. My at-sea duties often prevented me from attending church, so I started fellowship and discipleship programs aboard ship and on base with those I led to Christ.

In my last year in the Navy and for the two years before joining the Coast Guard, I spent all my free time spreading the Gospel to all who would listen among the unchurched in central Florida.

In June 1975, I married my best friend, Diane Gleason, from Cocoa Beach. But that's another story.[11]

I joined the Coast Guard in 1977. While at sea off the Oregon coast in February 1979, I was seriously injured during a search and rescue operation and flown by helicopter to a government hospital in Seattle. Several months later, they gave me a medical discharge with no intention of bringing resolution to my significant back and neck injuries. The trauma and subsequent disabilities ended my military career, and the physical consequences remain through the 24/7 pain I experience to this day.

But government service prepared me for later missions. In the Navy, I learned boldness in witness and how to live (incarnate) Jesus Christ before men in close quarters, exercising faith without shame. Luke 19:10 says that Jesus came to seek and save (Search and Rescue) the lost. In the Coast Guard, I learned search and rescue, laying down my life to rescue the lost at sea and those in peril.

God prepared me for missions in other ways as well. While serving with NOAA, I learned that my old Catholic seminary campus had been purchased by the Philadelphia College of Bible[12], and I promptly enrolled. In 1984, I earned my BS in Bible from the same campus where I had studied for the priesthood thirteen years before. From 1985 to 1992, six nights a week from

---

11. See "Brought Together" on page 39.

12. I attended Philadelphia College of Bible. When daughter Bonnie attended my alma mater, it was renamed Philadelphia Biblical University, and today it is Cairn University.

11:00 p.m. to 5:00 a.m., I walked the streets and alleys of an inner-city Philadelphia drug slum, ministering to drug gangs and street people. I held weekly midnight church meetings in a notorious crack house for those our Father called to Himself, and I was privileged to watch God miraculously transform a small army of young men and women.

All of these diverse experiences helped forge in me the physical, intellectual, and spiritual attributes I would need to endure the frigid climate of a lethally harsh environment among a strange people in an unfamiliar culture—all in the warmth of God's love and the cozy intimacy of His presence.

CHAPTER 3

Diane's Testimony

For we are His workmanship, created in Christ Jesus for good works, which God prepared beforehand that we should walk in them. —Ephesians 2:10

O N OCTOBER 10, 1951, I entered the world, the first child of a career Army officer then stationed at Fort Bliss Army Base in El Paso, Texas. Over the next 11 years, I was joined by two brothers and a sister. During those years, we followed Dad's deployments to Hungary, Canada, and five U. S. states, until my sophomore year in high school when he settled in Cocoa Beach, Florida and retired from the military to work for the Kennedy Space Center. Dad was a dedicated Anglican Catholic who, wherever and whenever he could, served the church. He did so in every level and position of lay leadership.

I came to the Lord and dedicated my life to missions in high school in 1965. A girlfriend invited me to her Pioneer Girls revival meeting near our home in Ottawa, Canada. There I heard Acts 4:12, a verse I had first encountered at Vacation Bible School in second grade: "Salvation is found in no one else, for there is no other name under heaven given to mankind by which we must be saved." For the first time, I accepted the truth that I was a sinner who had offended God and needed to repent and surrender all of myself to Him and His will for my life. That evening, I surrendered to Him. When I arrived home, I excitedly told my parents that I had "given my life to Jesus." Mom did not react; Dad was offended. They never accepted my leaving the Episcopal Church and its traditions to pursue a resolute adventure with God and Michael. Sadder still, they were never willing or able to join me in spontaneous worship or share in the hunger for the Bible that continued to grow in my lonely heart.

In 1970, in college, I was deeply touched by God's Holy Spirit. For Him to make me the most effective conduit of His love and grace to Sakha women, He had to address three key debilitating issues with me: pride, fear, and unbelief.

Pride: Dad was a West Point graduate and I grew up around army officers and their kids. We didn't interact with enlisted families. Dad was assistant military attaché in Hungary and later was on the cutting edge of developing aerospace communications with NASA. Mom was an honors graduate in Music from a prestigious university. From my third grade year, Mom and two renowned concert pianists trained me. I graduated second in my high school class and entered college on a full music scholarship. In all those years, I learned two things: how to play the piano really well and how to find my self-worth only in performance.

Fear: I was petrified of many things, the worst being failure. In music, and in life, I had to be perfect, and if I failed God or family, I could not face the consequences. My self-worth was so tied to performance that I could not grasp the wonderful truth that I was a sinner saved and sustained by grace, not by performance. Pride, performance, and failure together produced guilt, an unhealthy fear of God, fear of people, fear of imperfection, and fear that I could never measure up. These issues were aggravated by numerous sexual assaults against me in college and unable to find help and consolation in my parents. As I prepared to graduate fifth in my college class, the traumas and shame overwhelmed me.. I suffered two mental breakdowns resulting in hospitalizations and was misdiagnosed as manic-depressive.

Unbelief: My hospitalizations planted and watered an ugly seed of unbelief in me. The diagnosis fed a process of doubt and unbelief in my relationship with God. Did He really love me? Could I really trust Him? In the years to come, the problem grew as I faced many inexplicable trials. Ten years after college, I had two more breakdowns requiring hospitalization. How could my loving Father allow this to happen to me?

The first time Michael saw me was in 1972. I was in a padded cell of a mental health ward, but that day he saw me through God's eyes of agapé love, as he has for the 41 years since. Though he knows all of my issues, he has never wavered in his love. During the next 21 years, from our wedding day to our leaving for Siberia, we faced major challenges or traumas, each a test capable of destroying our faith, our family, and our marriage.

I will not fully chronicle the two decades of "hell," but the following give some idea of our continual challenges:

- Michael's two heart attacks and a severe injury at sea, with a medical discharge from the Coast Guard in 1979. He has never fully recovered from those injuries and they worsen as the years pass.

- The multiple rapes of our two oldest daughters as children by a ruling local church member and his two sons.

- The hurt of having 53 mailing addresses in 21 years, and never—even from childhood—settling down with close friends.

- The worry of never having enough money to take care of basic needs in affluent America.

- The trauma of a beloved Christian daughter going through a very painful divorce.

- The sudden deaths of my beloved little brother, father, and father-in-law.

- The nightmare of having a beloved Christian son living five years on heavy drugs and doing jail time.

After my fourth breakdown, in 1978, a doctor put me on high doses of lithium ... then I found I was pregnant with our only son. The doctor advised abortion, but that was out of the question for me, and I sternly refused. It was then we discovered that I have a severe form of reactive hypoglycemia. I must adhere to a specific healthy diet to maintain my mental and physical wellbeing.

I desperately sought stability in my life, as my spiritual walk was an emotional roller coaster based greatly on feelings and circumstances. One Sunday in 1981, while Michael was at sea, I was introduced to inductive Bible study through Kay Arthur's Precept Ministries. At the time, we had four small children and I had no transportation to a Bible study. So I ordered Kay's tapes and books and did the studies myself. My spiritual turning point was learning to listen to the Holy Spirit, through daily study and meditation on His Word, especially on Isaiah 26:3:

"You will keep him in perfect peace, whose mind is stayed on you: because he trusts in you."

God's Word began to transform and stabilize my life at a level I had never before experienced. I learned to rejoice in trials and to endure my hardships as a soldier of Christ. God taught me how to trust Him beyond my understanding. He taught me that in reality, faith is the substance of things hoped for, and the evidence of things I cannot see. I learned to value His great love for me, not based in my performance or life's circumstances. When I got really scared, He delivered me from fear and unbelief.

In 1984, I experienced the most devastating event in my life: an illegal hospitalization. Just before Michael finished Bible college in June, I contracted mononucleosis. When he graduated, we moved back to Florida, but Michael had to return to Pennsylvania for two weeks to finish a project. I was very weak, both physically and emotionally, and I knew I needed rest and help with my kids.

Rather than helping me, my dad saw an opportunity to commit me to a mental hospital against Michael's and my expressed will.

There is a very ugly, malevolent side to psychiatric malpractice in the U.S., and I became one of its victims on several occasions. My dad convinced a doctor that I was a serious schizophrenic, and the psychiatrist and hospital staff put me on dangerously high doses of a variety of anti-psychotic drugs without any medical testing. I was confined and abused for 17 days in a living hell, with no one to protect or rescue me.

My dad and the doctor were about to permanently commit me to a state mental institution, but Michael wrote the hospital president, warning that if I were not released at once, he would take my story to the press. Less than 24 hours later, I was released, but obscenely dumped on the sidewalk in front of the hospital, where I lay, bruised, bleeding, convulsing, drooling, and lactating—all from the drugs. Michael came for me, and for the next several weeks, he, his mom, and a sister helped me withdraw cold turkey from the powerful drugs. The convulsions stopped. Still, it took two years for my hormones to return to normal. My self-worth was completely destroyed, and I was unable to be whole and strong for my husband and my kids. I could not speak with my father for years after that.

Michael took charge of our home. He bought me attractive business attire and found an office job for me. I would never have chosen to work, but for the next 10 years, God restored my joy, and developed in me superb and much sought after office and computer skills.

Looking back, I see that God used that hospitalization to prepare me for Siberia. Because of my excellent computer, office, leadership, and training skills, I was invited to teach college-level computer English in Siberia, which answered our fervent prayers for a doorway to enter that region for ministry.

After years of learning forgiveness, I reconciled with my dad and enjoyed his company before he died in 1998.

I did not choose to enter corporate America, but there I, like Michael, learned the hurt, pain, and shame of working hard but not being able to meet basic financial obligations. After Michael suffered a second heart attack, I became the chief wage earner, and he raised our kids through their teen years. I cried to the Lord during those difficult years and did not understand the purpose of our hardships—until we went to Siberia.

Because of my experiences in the crucible, I could not in any way look down on those wonderful Sakha women or share Jesus with them from a platform of superiority. God walked with me in the pain, hurt, and indignity of 21 years so I could identify with them in the horrible shame and hardships of their lives. I could only reach their hearts out of humility, compassion, love, and true identification, the very qualities God worked in me though my many afflictions.

Though Michael and I suffered much in the U.S., especially through the cruelty of Christians, nothing could truly have prepared us for moving to a lethal and isolated region of northern Siberia with no promise of support. Those old waves of fear and unbelief returned. But in the middle of my deep grappling with inadequacy, fear, and doubt, God gently assured me, *"You're here because I want you here."* I didn't have to be all together, be the greatest teacher on the planet, or have my *all* my stuff together. Daily He showed me His love, tender care, and provision.

One morning, alone in our village, I felt a gripping, gnawing fear concerning our need for basic provisions. God spoke in my inner spirit, and I knew in that moment, though I couldn't see the provisions in front of me, I could choose to trust Him anyway. I audibly rebuked fear in the name of Jesus. Immediately the strangling bondage of the fear broke, and God gave me His sweet peace. We have experienced many such situations that allow us to trust in Him daily.

As I trust Him, He frees me from torment. His perfect love casts out fear. God has been pouring into my heart His love, and I rest in that perfect love. Fear is a great stronghold among the Sakha people.

They are daily threatened by and terrified of many things: evil spirits and their shamans, hunger, disease, bitter stinging cold, cruel and crooked police, and chronic violence and persecution. I have been privileged to show them—as God showed me—how to overcome great difficulties, and walk in peace and love in hard times and ostensibly impossible situations.

God blessed us with many friendships among the leading citizens of our Siberian region. Our home, situated at the crossroads of four large districts, became God's address for hospitality, provision, and Gospel proclamation. As an evangelist, church planter, and itinerant pastor among the Sakha villages of our deadly region, Michael faced many challenges and obstacles. Therefore, God called me to two vital tasks: to be a loving helpmeet to my husband, and to love and serve the Sakha women in faith and humility. I was not to defend my rights or expect humanitarian treatment. I was to trust God for our provision and pour out to those wonderful people the love that He poured into my heart.

Had I not been through His refining furnace for over two decades, I would not have identified with those precious Sakha hearts. God used the most hurtful things in my life as sturdy dark threads in a beautiful tapestry, to work a depth, compassion, and strength in me that ease and success never could have. If we could only grasp our Father's heart, we would better understand His purposes for us in tribulation (biblical Greek *thlipsis*: "pressure").

Yes, God had to break my pride, fear, and unbelief to use me in northern Siberia. His purpose was not to destroy me, but to remold me. He loves me so much, and I desire to be used of Him more and more as I am changed into the image of His dear Son.

Nothing can separate me from the love of God in Christ Jesus my Lord. Nothing. When my Heavenly Father looks at me, he ascribes no shame or condemnation to me. He sees me as His beloved child. He looks for those He can prepare to share His love to a lost and dying world. He woos His lost children out of every tribe and nation, by sending us, imperfect vessels who are nevertheless ready to answer His call. He uses those willing to be broken and reshaped into His image in the furnaces of affliction, to bring in the harvest of the ages. I thank the Lord for my life and all He has done to mold and bring me to this place of ministry.

* * *

I finished a master's degree in biblical counseling and it is my life's passion to serve the One who loves, heals, and transforms me through tribulations, that I might humbly serve His precious hurting ones. For I know that I am His workmanship created in Christ Jesus for good works which God prepared long ago for me to walk in.

Isaiah speaking of himself and of His Messiah (Isaiah 61:1–2), and Jesus quoting from Isaiah (Luke 4:18–19) in the synagogue:

> *"The Spirit of the Lord is upon Me,*
> *Because He has anointed Me*
> *To preach the gospel to the poor;*
> *He has sent Me to heal the brokenhearted,*
> *To proclaim liberty to the captives*
> *And recovery of sight to the blind,*
> *To set at liberty those who are oppressed;*
> *To proclaim the acceptable year of the Lord."*

At His last upper room meal, Jesus confessed to His Father in the hearing of His disciples:

> *"I have brought you glory on earth by completing the work you gave me to do … I have revealed you to those whom you gave me out of the world."*

Before history began, God chose Michael and me for a special end-time pioneer work among one of the most isolated and hurting people in the 21st century, and He put this least likely lady candidate through 21 years of strict training to get her there.

Such is my purpose.

My driving passion.

My mission.

CHAPTER 4

Brought Together

R B: I MET MICHAEL ("Dr. Mike" to me) and Diane Meagher in April, 2013, when he spoke at our church at the invitation of our pastor. After the service, I approached him, remarked that they "really should write a book" about their Siberian missions, and simply offered my services as a professional writer to help them get the book to a publisher.

Little did I know I was the "answer to three years of prayer." Even less did I realize that I would need to help write this book as much to build *my* faith as to encourage others in theirs.

During our times together preparing this book—including meetings, interviews, meals, social gatherings, and recreational diversions—I observed the Meaghers' relationship up-close and personal. They unwaveringly treat each other with the soft affection, sturdy respect, and kind and encouraging dialogue typically confined to newlyweds. Yet, though both approaching the proverbial "retirement age," the Meaghers' consistent display of love for each other has not ossified over the decades. I never saw or heard as much as a hint of harshness or irritation between them.

One can only surmise that their transparent, often wordless, mutual affection served as a door-opening preface to endear the hearts of the Sakha people and prepare them to receive the Good News of salvation by a supremely loving God. They truly are an embodiment of the Lord's exhortation in John 13:35: *"By this all will know that you are My disciples, if you have love for one another."*

RB: *Okay, let's cut right to the chase. How did you two meet?*

MM: Actually, there wasn't any chasing—with either of us. . Until I left the Catholic Church, female companionship wasn't even on my radar screen. It seemed that all my guy friends growing up practiced the arts of romance and wife hunting. I had never practiced those skills. As a new believer, I sensed in my spirit that Father had eventual marriage for me. As a Navy man, I was clueless how to go about accomplishing such a formidable task while at sea. Of the millions of females on the planet, how could I know which one He had for me? I humbly asked Him to find and bring the one He had for me as He had done with Isaac and Rebecca in Genesis 24. And He didn't wait long to give me His answer.

DM (giggling): The first time I saw Michael, he was wearing nothing but a bath towel!

MM (blushing): Well, yeah, but we're getting a little ahead of ourselves here.

DM: In February 1972, while I was a junior majoring in piano and organ at Rollins College in Winter Park, Florida, I was introduced to a lady who was holding weekly children's Bible studies in her home about 10 minutes from the college. One afternoon, after the Bible study, she asked me if I knew of anyone who could give weekly piano lessons to her two youngest daughters, then 8 and 9 years old. I agreed, and over the next few months, she and I developed a strong friendship as Christian sisters.

MM: Two weeks after they met, I received a letter from Mom at sea (I was on a Navy cruise from February 14 to December 11) that informed me that she had recently met and befriended a nice young Christian lady from Rollins College—an organ and piano major. Mom wrote she would like to pay the young lady $50 a month to tutor my two little sisters, and asked whether I'd be willing to foot the bill. I wrote Mom that I would be happy to be a blessing to her, the college student, and my sisters, and immediately arranged a monthly automatic withdrawal from my Navy pay to be sent to that young lady at Rollins.

DM: As you can imagine, that regular income meant a lot to a poor little coed. And I was intrigued who this mystery benefactor from across the waters might be.

MM: During that 11-month cruise, our ship docked in Athens, Greece, and I was granted a three-week leave in September, so I visited my family. Mom invited me to see someone in a hospital in Orlando. We entered the psychiatric ward and were directed to one of the padded cells. At Mom's request, I looked through the small porthole in the door, and my heart broke at the sight. There, in a straitjacket in the corner, lay a beautiful young lady, trembling, curled up in a fetal position. Mom said, "That's Diane, the girl you're paying to teach piano lessons."

I was overwhelmed with a sense of compassion and personal accountability, and right then I got down on one knee in front of the door and prayed, *"Heavenly Father, if You would have me be a help and a blessing to this woman, I dedicate myself to You in that task."* I left the hospital, that young lady heavy on my heart and at the top of my prayer list. A few days later I returned to my ship, now anchored in Spain, and finished out our cruise, docking in the U.S. on December 11.

One week later, I was visiting my family in Maitland, Florida on a four-day liberty pass. It was Monday, December 18, in the early afternoon, and I was alone in the house (Dad was at work, Mom was shopping, and my five younger siblings were in school). I had just stepped out of the shower when I heard the doorbell ring. Assuming one of my siblings, coming home from school, got locked out of the house, I wrapped myself with a bath towel and opened the door. There stood a *beautiful woman* with her boyfriend in tow, both of them in formal attire from a military ball. She smiled at me and, in an angelic voice, said, "Oh you must be Mike! I'm Diane!"

DM: Well, he made quite a first impression! He stared at me, his jaw dropped, and all he could say was, *"Y-You're Diane?!"*

MM: After a very awkward pause, I invited them into the living room and beat a hasty retreat to get dressed.

DM: When Michael returned, we talked for three hours about our lives in the framework of our love for Jesus. My boyfriend— he'd been my boyfriend since childhood—didn't share our faith, and just sort of receded from our consciousness. He really didn't say anything, and we didn't really notice his absence in the conversation.

MM: Over the next two years, we became best friends—nothing more. I had desired to be a Catholic priest all of my growing up years and had never considered having a girlfriend. I had a few friends who were girls, but there was never a pursuit of the opposite sex for romantic interests.

DM: Neither of us considered our times together as "dating." In early 1973 Michael was transferred to the USS R.H. McCard, a Destroyer home ported in Tampa, Florida. In January 1974 I graduated from Rollins College, and returned to Cocoa Beach to live with my parents and work. Virtually every weekend Michael was not at sea he spent with me in Cocoa Beach for all of February, 1973 through June, 1975.

MM: I describe those two years as a very special time getting to know a Christian sister who impressed me as a woman who, more than anything else, wanted to know and follow Jesus Christ with her life. I followed Diane to Cocoa Beach and visited her on the weekends, staying in the bedroom of her younger brother Tommy, who was enrolled at West Point.

DM: Michael was a kind and compassionate friend who brought encouragement without demands of any kind. I was so hungry to know about God and His Word, and was always filled with questions. Michael was always eager to discuss the things of God together with open Bibles and hearts. He put no expectations on me about dress-up, make up, or to be artificial in my interactions with him and I always felt safe with him alone.

MM: A year later in 1974 came "The Fatal Kiss" … One Friday night, I dragged a very tired body after a hard cruise to Diane's parents' home and lay on the living room floor as Diane played a soothing Bach etude left-handed ("Intermezzo in D Minor"). She then massaged my neck for a few moments (the first time I had ever received such a treatment). It was so calming. I got ready to retire to her brother's room for the night, and I stopped her in the living room doorway, aimed high, and closed my eyes to give her a peck on the forehead—as a sign of brotherly appreciation, you understand.

DM: I thought he missed and I raised my face to meet his lips with mine!

MM: Um, I was 22 and had never before experienced lip-lock. But from that moment our relationship *changed*. That Sunday at our favorite park I briefly discussed maybe bringing Diane down near my ship in Tampa, possibly renting a small mobile home or apartment for her and finding her a job, and perhaps she could help us with a small church plant. We parted ways that afternoon knowing we would not meet again for two weeks (my ship was shoving off the next morning for a two-week cruise to Cuba).

DM: And I parted ways wondering what he meant by all those plans for us in Tampa.

MM: I wrestled with the Holy Spirit the entire 84 miles back to the ship. Apparently, He was not going to let me be at peace until I asked Diane to marry me. I was upset that proposing to Diane would ruin a great friendship, and seriously doubted that I was worthy of being her husband.

I arrived at the pier about 7:00 p.m. but sat in my car until 11:30 that night, arguing with my Heavenly Father about how I *really* did not want to ask Diane to marry me. I finally cut a deal with God. I required Him to take the entire two-week cruise to work in me the intestinal fortitude to pop the question. As I walked the plank onto the ship, I promised that the next time I stepped back off I would go straight to Cocoa Beach and ask her.

I started work the next morning at 5:00, preparing the engine room for getting underway. At 10:30 a.m. we began to steam into the Gulf of Mexico. I performed my duties on autopilot, utterly flummoxed by the prospect of proposing to Diane two weeks hence. So I didn't hear the captain's announcement over the ship's main communication speaker. While the rest of the crew in my engine room were jumping and shouting for joy, and my mind was dully migrating from Cocoa Beach back to the ship, the captain finished his announcement with, " ... and before you leave the ship this afternoon, we will have a dress blue (uniform) inspection on the pier."

I immediately exploded, "Before we leave the ship?! WHY?!"

A shipmate rebuked me for not paying attention. While I was distracted by my reverie, one of the ship's main propellers was disabled by a main shaft bearing failure. The problem had been discovered and inspected during the three-mile trip to the Gulf. The cruise had been canceled, the ship would undergo a major repair that week, and after the aforementioned inspection, we were released for a three-day extended liberty.

I was devastated. God had tricked me into promising that I would ask Diane to marry me the next time I got off the ship. I thought that would be two weeks away, but He chose to ignore the condition I imposed upon Him. Now, only the next day after my promise, I was driving back to Cocoa Beach to make a fool of myself before Diane. Instead of changing into my civilian clothes, I stayed in uniform. It would be the first time Diane saw me in all of my military regalia, and I hoped that would perhaps help entice a positive response from her.

Just 23 hours after I left Diane, I was standing at her parents' front door in my dress blues asking in a trembling voice if she would accompany me to our favorite Italian restaurant by the beach. On our way to the restaurant I explained the ship's problem, which caused my surprise early return. But I decided I would wait to pop the question over steak and lobster.

I parked and turned off the car. As I prepared to get out and open her door, she exclaimed with a broad smile and a twinkle in her eye, "Oh, by the way, I asked my dad and my pastor and they both said it's okay for me to marry you!"

DM: Well, I thought when he was talking about getting a trailer and moving me to Tampa, that was his way of proposing marriage! That's what it sounded like to me. I thought it was kind of fast, but I wrote a quick "Dear John" letter to my childhood friend who was still pursuing me. That night I called my pastor and sat down with my dad and both of them were very pleased by Michael's proposal and gave me their blessing.

MM: Only then did it make sense to me why the Holy Spirit insisted that I "ask"—because in Diane's mind and understanding I already had. Oh yes, and I *really* enjoyed my steak and lobster that night!

DM (chuckling): I don't remember what I had.

DM: we determined during our engagement that we would like to have four children, and to have them before my 30th birthday. I got pregnant on our honeymoon. On our 5th wedding anniversary I gave birth to our fourth and final child in our tiny home on wheels in the Olympic Mountains of Washington State, four months shy of my 29th birthday.

RB: *What was home life like while the kids were growing up?*

MM: For most of their childhood years, our kids grew up in school buses I had converted into "rolling homes." I'm grateful for Diane's faith when I asked her about living in a bus. I was so relieved at her answer. You remember what you said, honey?

DM: I just said, "Make it pretty."

MM: For the most part, the kids loved it. They also enjoyed helping me work on the buses. Each one of our children learned very early how to use saws, hammers, measuring tapes, etc. Another advantage was that the buses and all improvements were paid for before we moved in. We never had to make a mortgage payment.

DM: Of course, it was easier when the children were small. When they reached high school, they were more concerned about their privacy and personal space. But we always had a bathroom, shower, full kitchen, and we made sure each of our children had their own bunk area with a privacy curtain and a reading light. And there was always room at the dinner table for everyone.

MM: Every bus—I call them, ahem, works of art on wheels—also had running water, electricity, air conditioning, and heat, pretty much everything a Class A motor home would have. Well, I take that back. We also had stained glass! And I built everything to even higher safety standards than those imposed on the RV industry. I maximized the living space, too. On each bus I raised the whole roof by eighteen inches and all storage was built up and out of the way, like the overhead compartments in an airplane, and the entire home was designed to be kid-friendly. Those who see smaller space as child neglect don't realize that with some foresight and ingenuity space can be maximized without sacrificing quality of life.

DM: With every school our children attended, when word got where they were living, their schoolmates would flock to see our home, and we always welcomed them. Sometimes it was hard to corral four kids in three different schools, but children were good at helping take care of one another.

MM: And most of the kids wanted to trade places with our children!

DM: That's right, and even without us ever having had a television. We never lacked for things to do, and the kids never lacked for food, clothes, shelter, love ...

MM: ... or entertainment. Diane is a musician and I'm a graphic artist. We regularly held classes on those subjects. Also, I would do vaudeville, and Diane and I would sing and dance to the tunes of the

50s and 60s. We kept plenty of books around and there was always something to do. No one ever got bored.

But one of our best family times was playing "wallyball" in our 18' x 7-1/2' living room. I had installed eyehooks to stretch a net across the room. We all lay on the floor (one parent and two kids per side) and batted a Nerf ball back and forth over the net, smacking the ball as hard as we could and using the walls and ceiling as need be.

DM: The one rule was that no one could lift their head from the floor.

RB: *How did others react to your intentional living arrangements?*

MM: Well, we never said it was for everyone. We were simply being prepared for a sacrificial lifestyle on the mission field. But our critics imposed their own standards on our family, and sometimes they weren't very complimentary. I think they were just projecting their fear that God might ask them to do it, too.

DM: But others were very curious and inquisitive about our lifestyle.

MM: That's right. Quite often, we'd stop somewhere for gas or to stretch our legs, and we'd get delayed for 45 minutes or more as curiosity seekers requested tours of our strange digs. Of course, we took that opportunity to tell them about our lives and our ministry, and regularly ended up sharing the Gospel with them.

DM: We donated three of the four buses to mission boards. We traded the other one for a four-bedroom house in Orlando. For the first few nights in the house, the kids were scared of big space and they all slept together in one room. They were afraid to go in the back bedrooms.

RB: *When did you realize you were called to Siberia? How did you find out?*

MM: In 1994, when I was a second-year M.Div. student at Reformed Theological Seminary in central Florida, I browsed the campus ministry bulletin board and saw an invitation for a short term mission trip to Russia. Intrigued, I joined the expedition—and that started the dominoes of divine appointments that culminated in our call there. Diane and I had both answered personal missionary calls in our teens. We talked quite a bit about that from the time we first met, and after we married, together we kept our spiritual eyes and ears open for where God might call us.

God used my injury and discharge in 1979 to begin training us for missions. After two weeks of fasting and prayer that year, Diane and I resolved to begin radical preparations for foreign missions. From our experiences in other countries in our separate pasts, we knew that the places God could call us to would not have the well-to-do lifestyles we grew up with or enjoyed in our first five years of marriage. It was easy to say that we would go and serve Him anywhere, but could we really do it? We were also challenged concerning our love for God. Was our love for Him based on all the good things we expected from His hand, or on who He is, regardless of what we had? Did we love God or His gifts? We were challenged by Job 1:9–11.[13] If we had nothing, would we still love Him? Our Father touched our hearts deeply with the promises of Matthew 19:29[14] and John 12:25-26[15].

DM: It took us a year to give away nearly all of our possessions, and at times it was rather painful. But we committed ourselves to a system of disposing of our property. We took all the items we

---

13. *So Satan answered the LORD and said, "Does Job fear God for nothing? Have you not made a hedge around him, around his household, and around all that he has on every side? You have blessed the work of his hands, and his possessions have increased in the land. But now, stretch out Your hand and touch all that he has, and he will surely curse You to Your face!"*

14. *And everyone who has left houses or brothers or sisters or father or mother or children or lands, for my name's sake, will receive a hundredfold and will inherit eternal life.*

15. *Whoever loves his life loses it, and whoever hates his life in this world will keep it for eternal life. If anyone serves me, he must follow me; and where I am, there will my servant be also. If anyone serves me, the Father will honor him.*

owned but hadn't used or looked at for the previous six months, and stowed them in a back room in the house. Whatever we didn't go in and retrieve out of necessity during the next six months we gave away. That emptied the room and lifted the burden of those material things from our lives.

MM: In 1981, with no debt and only the barest of possessions, we continued our experiment in simplicity. We traded our only car for a dilapidated 1951 school bus that would serve as our home. We lived that summer with our four children (aged one to five years old) in a friend's dilapidated goat shed at the base of Washington State's Olympic Mountains until our school bus was livable.

DM: A related commitment we made was to eat as naturally and healthfully as we could. No family trips to McDonald's, no boxes and bags of junk food stuffing the cupboards (which we didn't have anyway), no commercially processed easy-to-prepare meals full of preservatives and other toxins. Michael bought me a grain mill, and we made our own bread. I committed myself to learning as much as I could about preparing all natural whole foods for our family meals, and trained myself to dispense all natural herbal remedies in place of manufactured drugs whenever anyone in the family needed treatment. We sustained ourselves from the harvest of a personal garden whenever we could.

MM: I combined my lifelong art and craft skills with my marine mechanic expertise from the Navy and Coast Guard to convert the bus into a cozy home for six. Eighteen years later our youngest child graduated high school and moved out of our fourth bus home. Our last "house on wheels" location was in Longwood, FL, where we moved in 1994 so our four children could finish high school and I could attend Reformed Theological Seminary. From 1994 to 1996, I did evangelism on the campus of the University of Central Florida as we prepared for Siberia.

DM: We had committed not to leave for missions work until all our children were raised and had moved out of our home.

MM: God really prepared us well. In June 1996, we received a call from a Russian man charged with finding us a residence in Siberia. He was very distressed that he could only find us housing too small for Americans—only 250 square feet. We really brightened his day when we told him that his provision was perfect, as it was 10 square feet *larger* than our comfortable school bus home. God is so wonderful!

CHAPTER 5

Raymond's Testimony

I AM, BY NEARLY EVERY ACCOUNT, an ordinary guy. I wasn't plucked out of a street gang or healed of a fatal disease, and upon my passing, over six billion of my fellow earthly inhabitants will take no notice whatsoever of the event.

Born in Cleveland, Ohio (and thus, congenitally, a perennially frustrated sports fan), and raised in Fort Wayne, Indiana, I have never spoken with an accent or lived among a people who did. My favorite singing group is the Beach Boys, I prefer Norman Rockwell to almost any other artist, and I still enjoy reruns of *The Andy Griffith Show* whenever I can.

I was, in the words of Garrison Keillor, "marvelously adequate" as a student in our parochial grade school, public junior high and high schools, the Fort Wayne commuter campus of Indiana University, and Valparaiso Law School. I usually minded my own business, mixed just enough study with too much extracurricular activity, and pretty much got along with everyone who got along with me.

I was never the best—or the worst—at anything. I am stymied by all things mechanical, my singing voice can kill small game at 20 yards, and even though I grew up in the Hoosier state, basketball just isn't my game. I have, however, been blessed with a fair degree of wit and humor, an above average flair for putting words and sentences together, and a driving passion to study, teach, and write.

In sum, I am totally, entirely, absolutely unique—just like everybody else.

My religious life was average, too, I suppose. I (sometimes willingly, sometimes as a hostage) accompanied my family to the Sunday morning services at our rural Lutheran church, dutifully sat through the sermons and litanies, and dropped the obligatory something into the offering plate. I didn't smoke, drink, or mess around with women, and I was blissfully content to float on spiritual autopilot.

Until I met Mike Schlatter. He appeared on campus during my sophomore year of college, always upbeat, invariably passing out Gospel tracts and pocket New Testaments, and telling everyone who would listen about Jesus, usually in a discourse generously riddled with "Praise the Lord!"s and "Hallelujah!"s.

I was no different than many of the other students who diligently tried to avoid him, but for one reason or another, I was seldom able to generate sufficient escape velocity to dodge his gravitational pull. I had always been taught to tolerate those who were different from me, so I politely endured his sermonettes, asked a few superficial questions to corroborate my façade of interest, and eventually departed, successfully unaffected by his evangelistic efforts. Or so I thought ...

The more we talked, the more I found myself sipping the unfamiliar but intriguing truth he temperately and respectfully offered for my consideration. By the end of the semester, we had become friends, though I was still guarded against his religious fervor.

One day, Mike asked me for a ride home. I drove him to his small and spare second-floor apartment near downtown Fort Wayne. As I sat at the little Formica table in the kitchen, he brought out a couple bowls from the cupboard, opened the freezer, and retrieved a half-gallon carton of butter pecan ice cream.

I was stunned by this spiritually incongruous frivolity. "You eat ice cream?!" I stammered. "I thought you were a Christian!"

Mike shrugged his shoulders, smiled at me, and said with a matter-of-factness that jolted me more than his words, "God gives me the money, and I enjoy it." Funny how, among the thousands of words Mike spoke to me, those are the only ones I still recall verbatim.

Mike was incessantly inviting me to this revival or that crusade or some outreach or another. But he batted zero for the year, as I always had an excuse, real or contrived, to avoid attending them.

Mike's call the July after my sophomore year started the same as always. This time he wanted me to attend a Teen Challenge program at one of the churches in Fort Wayne.

"What day?" I asked.

"Tonight," he replied.

Aha! Today was Thursday! I had a readymade—and honest—reason to decline. One of the Lutheran churches in town held Thursday night services to accommodate parishioners who spent summer weekends at the lake. I wouldn't actually be lying if I said I was thinking of going to that church.

But before I could speak my regrets, Mike sweetened the pot with an offer I found difficult to decline: "If you come to the meeting tonight, I'll never ask to go to another one."

What to do? I told Mike I would think about it and call him back. I went to my bedroom to mull the options, and after some rumination, decided to do the most spiritual thing I could think of ...

I pulled a quarter from my pocket and determined that heads meant the church service and tails meant the Teen Challenge meeting. I gave the coin a flip and watched it bounce around on the wooden floor. It came up tails. So, I did the second most spiritual thing I knew: tried best two out of three ... then three out of five ...

Upon the fourth consecutive tails, I figured God was trying to tell me something, so I called Mike and told him I'd go to the meeting.

"That's great!" he said. "I'll pick you up about six."

"No, no!" My response was immediate. "I mean," I said, modulating my voice, "I'll drive and meet you there."

Mike greeted me at the door and we walked into the building together. The meeting was being held in a gymnasium equipped with a makeshift raised altar, complete with podium, movie screen, and communion railing. Rows of folding wooden chairs were arranged the length of the gym.

I quickly memorized the locations of the emergency exits as I took a seat about two-thirds of the way back. Mike took the chair to my immediate left, and a married couple, fellow students of his religious ilk, sat directly behind me. Two empty chairs completed the row to my right.

The program featured *Please Make Me Cry,* a short movie about the life and conversion of drug addict and female gang member Cookie Rodriguez. After the film, a gentleman took the podium, asked everyone to bow their heads and close their eyes, and said, "If any of you felt something stir inside you from watching the film, please raise your hand."

I had felt something—something beyond the mere emotional reaction to a warm and touching story—but I wasn't sure what it was. So when I felt my right arm unconsciously begin to levitate, I didn't stop its ascent. Apparently a few others had also raised their hands, as the speaker acknowledged their responses. When my arm was fully raised, the man looked right at me (somehow I knew, even though my eyes were shut) and gently said, "God bless you, fella."

Really? What a kind and gracious personal benediction from a man who didn't even know me. I did feel blessed.

I figured they'd now wrap up the show, dismiss the assemblage, and I could go home with memories of a positive, encouraging experience.

But neither they nor God were finished for the night. We were instructed to open our hymnals to "Amazing Grace" and the speaker prefaced the singing with an exhortation: "All of you who raised your hands are invited to come down to the altar." Come to the altar? For what? I had raised my hand; wasn't that enough? I deemed the gesture of going forward unnecessary, and was ready to call it a night, but felt it rude to leave before the song was over.

About halfway through the first verse, I felt a gentle nudge in my left side. *No, Mike, don't push me,* I thought, and slowly turned toward him to quietly murmur that caution. He was singing, eyes closed, face tilted upward, with his arms raised in worship. *Pretty slick,* I mused, *giving me a shove and then adopting that pious posture.*

The speaker repeated his invitation and directed the musicians to lead the audience in another verse. Again, halfway through the verse, I felt the kidney punch, a little harder this time. Rather annoyed, I immediately wheeled toward Mike—and found him still enraptured in worship. I turned to the couple behind me, thinking they too would be capable of such a stunt, but the rows were far enough apart that they couldn't reach me, and they were embracing each other around the waist while holding a hymnal with their free hands. None of them had laid a finger on me—but I was unmistakably touched.

My hands began to sweat and I waited impatiently for the singing to end so I could beat a hasty retreat. But the man up front took the microphone again and said, "We're going to sing one more verse to give you a chance to come forward."

This time, only two notes into the verse, I was pushed with such force that I had to take a step to the right to maintain my balance. At that instant, I made the choice to take another step ... and then another ... and another ... I reached the end of the row, stepped into the side aisle, and found myself jogging to the altar.

When I reached the communion rail, I plopped to my knees, squeezed my eyes shut, and knelt motionless, trying to grasp what was happening. Immediately, a fellow I would never see parked himself next to me and asked, "What's the matter, fella? What do you need?"

"I don't know," I truthfully replied. "I go to church and live a decent life. But there's just, I don't know," I haltingly confessed, "something missing."

"Do you need assurance, is that it?"

"Yeah, I guess so."

"Okay, just say this prayer with me ... " and he led me in what many refer to as The Sinner's Prayer. Just as I finished parroting his words, I felt a tingle in my forehead, right along my hairline. It grew in intensity as it accelerated down my face and neck. When the tingle reached heart level, it flushed through me with such a "whoosh" that I reflexively gasped and breathed an astonished "Wow!"

"What happened?" my anonymous acquaintance asked. I described the feeling and its journey, and he gleefully chirped the diagnosis: "You've been saved! Hallelujah! Okay, now repeat after me: 'Thank you, God.'"

"Thank you, God."

"Thank you, Jesus."

"Thank you, Jesus."

"Now just keep praising the Lord," he instructed. So I did, clumsily, I suppose, in the best way I knew how. At some point, my ringside companion left, and I continued to thank God for what I felt was an appropriate length of time.

I got up to go back to my seat, opened my eyes, turned around, and ...

The gym was dark and quiet. The speaker, musicians, and crowd had left. The chairs were all folded and stacked on carts along the side walls. A single exit light shone over the back door, where my friends were quietly, smilingly waiting for me.

I had been kneeling at the altar for 45 minutes, oblivious to the world I had temporarily left behind. I had no idea where I had been during that time.

Yes, my life changed that night, though the full ramifications are yet to be seen. I still, like before, succeed and fail, laugh and cry, start and stop. But that night, God instilled in me a new spirit that makes my life, my paradigm now, as dimensionally different from the old me as a sculpture differs from a painting.

Years later, I asked God, "Where was I for those 45 minutes? Please show me if you want to." And before me He unfolded a mental image. On a majestic throne sat a large and powerful God. I was nestled in his bosom as He gently stroked my hair and whispered Fatherly comforts to me.

"You were in my lap," He said.

And someday I'll be there again. Meantime, I'm asking Him to reveal what He was whispering in my ear that night ...

Since my second birth on July 17, 1975, my mission field has consisted primarily of a chair, a desk, and my computer keyboard. Throughout the decades, I have studied, written, and taught about Him and His rich, persistent mercies.

As I exercised those gifts, God has honed in me the ability to write, proofread, and edit—articles, columns, blogs, studies, and books. Each literary product helped prepare me for the next. In fact, my two most recent books—a compilation of devotionals and a chronicle of the adventures and spiritual recommitment of a professional wilderness tour guide—helped forge the skills necessary to write a book about two missionaries sent by God to Siberia ...

CHAPTER 6

God's Sovereign Hopscotch

WELCOME TO THE "BLACK HOLE," in many ways the most inhospitable place on the globe. Located in Siberia's Sakha Republic, it is a region used as a nuclear test site and as a toxic waste dump for more than 40 years; the harmful effects of which still linger at dangerous levels throughout the area. Brutal weather conditions, short growing seasons, and lack of commercial opportunities and essential medical care add to its inhabitants' woes.

One early summer night in 1998, missionary Michael Meagher endured a rough three-day, 400-mile trip from his home in Yakutsk along unpaved roads into the region as one of 53 people sardined aboard a 1950s 30-passenger bus. His goal: smuggle himself in and out of Vilyuysk—getting caught by authorities for making the unauthorized trip he was warned could mean death—to get a half-day reconnaissance peek at the area he and his wife, Diane, felt called to as their new Christian mission field.

His travel companions included four professors and four dozen students from the Vilyuysk Pedagogical College who conspired to keep his presence a secret. Meanwhile, Diane stayed behind and earnestly prayed for her husband's protection in a place where outsiders—especially Christians—were not welcome.

Michael was spirited into the home of a complicit villager for an overnight stay. For eight hours after they finished dinner at 7:00 p.m., he and the man of the house fellowshipped and laughed, communicating solely through Michael's cartoon depictions of his life and family in America.

At 3:00 a.m., the men were interrupted by a pounding on the door. Sure he had been betrayed, Michael breathed, "Yes, Father, I'm dead. This is exactly what I was warned about before I left." He hustled to his room, dropped to his knees beside his bed, reviewed his sin accounts with God, and asked Him to get Diane safely back to the States. The visitor, a messenger representing the regional governor, told the homeowner that Michael had an 8:00 a.m. appointment with the governor.

When he and his interpreter were ushered into the governor's office, Michael offered a silent prayer and extended his hand to introduce himself. To his amazement, the governor responded by stepping forward from behind the massive desk, shaking Michael's hand, and saying with a smile, "You don't need to tell me your name. I know who you and your wife are. How may I help?"

The governor explained that, during the Meaghers' years in Yakutsk, word had spread across the republic of the American couple who had devoted themselves to loving the Sakha people with great affection and kindness as they taught business and computers to the next generation.

The second reason for the governor's graciousness was historical. In 1890, Kate Marsden, a young British nurse in the Crimean War, rode to St. Petersburg and asked the czar where she could be the most help. He recommended the Vilyuysk region, whose people had recently suffered an outbreak of leprosy. Accompanied only by a native guide, Marsden went to Vilyuysk and started a desperately needed leper colony. Today, she is among the most honored and beloved women in that region.

The governor told Michael, "I have heard through reliable sources that you and Diane are blessing the Sakha in the name of the same Jesus that Kate Marsden served 100 years ago. If you are here in the name of this Jesus, you are welcome to purchase a home in Vilyuysk and live and work here as long as you wish."

When Michael walked in the door of their house in Yakutsk, Diane took one look at his face and said, "We're moving to Vilyuysk, aren't we?"

The Meaghers set about to buy one of only two houses for sale in the region. The larger of the two was a two-story log cabin with five bedrooms, with an asking price of $5,000 U.S., an unachievable purchase on the Meaghers' combined income of $40 a week.

Trusting in the power of corporate prayer, Michael and Diane e-mailed the few people outside immediate family who knew that they had moved to Siberia. They asked them to pray, "God, were You speaking through those divine appointments in Vilyuysk?"

The answer came quickly. A retired Washington, D.C. couple the Meaghers barely knew cashed in a federal retirement account to pay for the house. At the same time, close friends who pastored a small church in Italy that served American serviceman raised enough funds to move the Meaghers' possessions up the Lena and Vilyuy rivers to the new residence and to buy appliances and enough wood and tools to make furniture.

Now settled in Vilyuysk—debt and mortgage free—Michael and Diane immediately encountered the threats of a handful of powerful opponents, all of whom wanted them to "get out" of the region—dead or alive—and each of whom could have ended the Meaghers' work with little effort and no repercussions.

Yet, after two years, the Meaghers were still alive and thriving in their ministry. "Why?" they wondered.

Their answer came at a dinner party.

One of Russia's most joyous annual celebrations is the commemoration of the end of the "Great War" (World War II). In their second year in Vilyuysk, the Meaghers were invited to march in the grand parade and attend a VIP-only dinner party. After a series of speeches (which were translated in real time to the Meaghers), the Sakhas' most revered and decorated Soviet Army hero, a highly decorated sniper on the Nazi front, stepped to the podium for the evening's keynote address. Because of his revered standing, translation was not permitted during his speech. The Meaghers would have to wait to understand the hero's remarks.

The long and impassioned speech was frequently punctuated with rhetorical crescendos. In each such instance, the hero would look at Michael and Diane and grin widely. In response, the audience burst into thunderous applause. The Meaghers recognized some of those applauding as their sworn enemies. After his speech, the war hero, approached the Meaghers and vigorously shook their hands, repeatedly exclaiming: *"Ba-heeb-ba! Ba-heeb-ba!"* (Sakhali for "Thank you! Thank you!")

The translator then began to summarize the speech. "He spoke of an extraordinary occurrence in the Great War."

"But direct accolades to us?" the Meaghers asked. "We were born after our dads' war was over!"

In response, the translator recounted the hero's remarks:

"During what was considered the worst winter of the Great War, heavily armed contingents of the Soviet Army entered Vilyuysk and commanded everyone to prepare to die. They and their region were being sacrificed for the war effort. The army then stripped the people of all necessary provisions—food, clothing, petrol, vehicles, weapons, blankets, currency, gold, and silver—and the people were left to die, likely in a matter of days or weeks.

"Allied nations heard of the plan and offered to intercede, but Stalin refused help and forbad any rescue attempts, declaring that it was no other country's business how he dealt with his people.

"But someone in the American Pentagon defied Stalin's diktat and made a command decision, ordering two U.S. Army Air Corps bombers from a base in north-central China to sneak under Soviet

radar and cross into central Siberia. Those bombers made a "soft-drop" into Vilyuysk of many tons of sugar and flour in cotton and burlap sacks. A large number of locals survived that winter, subsisting on the sugar and flour and making articles of clothing and foot wraps from the sack material."

The translator closed his summary where the hero concluded his speech, with a non-negotiable edict to the audience: *"I remind everyone in this place, whether you like the American couple, are uncaring, or hate them, the grateful people of Vilyuysk are going to continue to honor and thank the American people and their country's military for saving us in a great act of sacrifice and love. For as long as this couple, Michael and Diane, are among us, we, the Sakha, will treat them as the officially protected and honored recipients of our appreciation."*

After the war hero left, a tiny elderly and frail lady, walking with much difficulty, approached the Meaghers. With tears of joy streaming down her cheeks, her countenance beamed with elation and appreciation. She pantomimed as if there were words written across her chest. She embraced the Americans and uttered her own series of *"Ba-heeb-ba"*s.

Through the translator, she told her story:

"I remember it all very clearly. I was a small girl in grade school when my momma made me a blouse of cotton and a burlap vest. The vest was printed with the English word SUGAR."

At that, the Meaghers and their translator joined the little lady in a flood of tears they had no desire to hide or stop.

Thus, at least three times in history, the God of Heaven visited Siberia's infamous "Black Hole" with His kind and benevolent sovereignty to ready them for His glorious Gospel message.

Part II:
The Story
(As Told Through a Series of Vignettes)

CHAPTER 7

Cartooning as Offense and Defense

BEGINNING IN JUNIOR HIGH SCHOOL, 1964, and continuing throughout my lifetime, wherever I go (especially when I am unable to communicate in a local language) ...

I was 12 years old when, one summer day, my dad opened a window for a one-time-only glance into a unique part of him. Though the window remained shuttered before then and ever since, that one brief peek profoundly changed my life.

I entered his study and found him hunched over his desk, deep in concentration. I edged closer and found that he was sketching a World War II era German sailor. The detail and precision were remarkable. Also on the desk lay decades-old depictions of U. S. and Japanese sailors, graced with equally accurate particularity.

Dad turned to me, smiled, and without a word handed me a thick old leather folder. I opened the treasure that I held in my hands only that one time, and with delightful curiosity and wonder, I reverently paged through perhaps 50 pages of sketches Dad had drawn when he was in his twenties: military ships, aircraft, tanks, field artillery—all drawn with the splendid technical detail of an expert mechanical draftsman sketching his first-hand experiences.

In that moment, my two dads—one heavenly, one human—gave me a precious lifetime gift, and for the next nine years, I devoted myself to countless hours of honing my skills in the visual arts.

My artistry would serve as my constant companion during difficult times in my junior high years. My neighbors, classmates, and siblings unanimously declared me too small, ugly, dumb, shy, uncoordinated, uncool, and—worst of all—awkwardly left-handed, to receive their respect, and for the next several years, they played the cast of judge, jury, and executioner in carrying out their verdict. I was ridiculed daily, and had nowhere to turn for surrogate friendship; Dad scorned family television viewing—and personal computers, the Internet, video games, and cell phones had not yet been invented.

So, beginning in seventh grade, I sentenced myself to solitary confinement at a secluded table in the school library with a pencil, sketchpad, and dozens of assorted illustrated books for reference and inspiration. Without the distraction of either a social or a sports life, I devoted many hours a day to emulating my Dad in the skill of pencil sketching.

One morning I drafted my favorite subject: a Trojan warrior in attack stance with full battle regalia. Just as I was finished the drawing, the most popular boy—and meanest bully—in our grade approached me to deliver his obligatory daily torment. Instead, he saw the newly created warrior and shattered the library's silence with a robust, "Whoa, that is so groovy!" I immediately handed him the sketch as a peace offering.

That was the last day I ever sketched alone in that school. I had a perpetual audience, and later that year, I was moved to a central table in the library by popular demand. During the rest of my junior high years, I gained a new "friend" with each piece of special request art I gave away. Each drawing carried a note of hope, friendship, and often humor, and art quickly became my preferred means of sharing with others.

I would later—and still do—present the Gospel and other Bible truths through simple pencil drawings. This proved immensely helpful in communicating with the Sakha people, long before I attempted their language.

CHAPTER 8

In the Bilges

1972–1973, aboard the
U.S.S. Franklin D. Roosevelt ...

D URING MY FIRST SIX MONTHS aboard the ship, I had two jobs, one I was trained for and one thrust upon me as a lesson for the future.

First, as a marine mechanic, I was assigned to the Number Three Engine Room, where I worked as part of the team that kept the third of four propellers turning; I also provided steam to the starboard catapult for launching aircraft.

Second, I was ordered to clean, scrape, and paint the bilges, the lowest—and hottest—part of the ship's engineering spaces where everything dirty, smelly, disgusting, and putrid fell, to be eventually pumped into the sea. In my opinion, it was the worst possible job aboard a warship.

I was not alone in that assessment. One morning, about 2 a.m., I was scraping the bilges when I heard the sound of boots marching toward me. I turned to see three Marines, armed with pistols, clubs, and automatic assault rifles, escorting five malefactors from the ship's brig to serve their punishment by—sitting next to me and scraping the bilges.

My morale plummeted lower than it ever had before. I was trying my best to be a faithful Christian, and was sharing my faith with the men aboard ship. I was a good sailor, not causing my superiors angst, obediently following orders with as much joy as I could muster. *God,* I asked, *I have a job considered punishment by the rest of the crew?*

I would finally realize His answer 24 years later.

I had been asking Him to prepare me to someday be the missionary He wanted me to be. And He had already determined to send Diane and me to Siberia's "Black Hole" region: the place prisoners were sent for ultimate punishment.

So He wasn't angry with me, and He wasn't punishing me.

He was merely answering my prayers.

CHAPTER 9

A Lake of Fire

February 23, 1973, Dockside, Naval Station, Mayport, Florida ...

O F COURSE I WAS ANGRY. I had every right to be. I was only obeying the Lord, after all, to share the Gospel with my shipmates in the engine room. My only motive was to help rescue them from the lake of fire that awaited them if they didn't turn to Jesus.

And what did I get in return? Mocking and derision. Those men weren't interested in hearing the salvation message, and they took every opportunity to let me know in the cruelest terms.

I stormed out of the engine room with their vile invectives ringing in my ears. I stopped on a nearby catwalk to fume for a few minutes, and then I tromped down the passageway, immersed in a pity party in which I was the host, guest of honor, and only invitee.

But God has a way of crashing such parties ...

The aircraft carrier U.S.S. *Franklin D. Roosevelt* was docked for maintenance and rehabilitation. One project was resurfacing the deck of Hangar Bay 1 (an enclosed area the size of two professional basketball courts located under the flight deck at the bow of the ship) with a nonskid tar and distillate mixture. During application, the substance and the fumes it emits are extremely flammable, and meticulous cautionary restrictions were imposed to avoid combustion. The deck was crosshatched with 4-foot wide walkways of heavy paper to allow foot travel during the procedure.

Still consumed in my pity party, I had just traversed one of the paper pathways along one edge of the bay. Barely two steps outside the bay's forward most hatch, I was slammed against the opposite bulkhead (wall) by a blast of hot air accompanied by a deafening "woof." My senses thoroughly jarred by the impact, I scrambled to my feet, turned back to look inside the bay—and absorbed in horror the sights and sounds of a hell no movie could ever adequately reproduce. A civilian dock worker had carelessly flicked a lit cigarette butt onto the deck. Thick, vicious flames were licking the 20-foot ceiling. Above their roar, I heard the screams of some two dozen terrified shipmates. Men who had moments before walked the paper pathways without concern were shrieking pleas for rescue.

I could see several of the men amid the inferno. One was flailing about. Another had thrown himself to the deck in a futile effort to dodge the heat and flames. Some were desperately looking about for an escape. None of them had their wits about them. They held the grotesque look of unmitigated panic. The scene haunts me to this day.

An officer grabbed me from behind, gave me an oxygen mask and asbestos gloves, and ordered me to run up a nearby stairway to rescue any shipmates trapped in the bunk area immediately above the bay. The flames were capable of warping the door of the bunk area, thereby sealing the victims inside to be roasted to death. As I rushed up the metal stairway, my footsteps became more labored. I looked down to see the rubber soles of my shoes melting to the steps.

I was able to open the bunk area door, freeing the captives. The firefighting mechanisms strategically mounted around the bay were activated and doused the flames within two minutes of the initial ignition. Miraculously, no life was lost, though many sailors suffered burns, some critical.

I will never forget the lesson of coming face-to-face with a lake of fire. I quickly repented of my self-pity and renewed my vow to obey God's command to preach His life-saving Gospel in season and out.[16]

---

16. Jude 22-23

CHAPTER 10

Driving a Cadillac to the Throne

April 1973, Norfolk, Virginia to Orlando, Florida ...

DURING MY FIRST TWO YEARS in the Navy, I hitch-hiked everywhere, as I didn't own a car.

In April 1973, our ship pulled into port for repairs in Norfolk, Virginia, and I decided to take a six-day pass and visit my family in Maitland.

I walked to I-95 and put out my thumb, praying, as always: *"Lord, please give me an escort who is seeking You, who needs to know You. Please give me someone to talk to who is ready to receive Your Gospel message."* Shortly, a brand-new 1973 Cadillac (the purchase stickers were still posted on the windows) pulled off the road to pick me up.

As I approached the car, the driver, a distinguished looking, smartly dressed gentleman, lowered the passenger side electric window and asked: "Do you have a gun?"

"No, sir," I immediately answered.

"Are you carrying a knife or any other weapon?"

"No, sir," I repeated.

"Any drugs?"

Upon my third "No, sir," he invited me to hop in the car.

After I was seated and we were on our way, He asked, "Where are you going, sailor?"

"Sir," I said. "I'm heading down to see my family in the Orlando area. Thank you for giving me a ride."

He said he needed some company for his trip down to Miami and that he would be happy to drop me off wherever I needed to go in Orlando.

Before long, the conversation turned to Vietnam. "Why is it," he mused aloud with some consternation, "that our powerful global military force can't overcome a comparatively small Communist force in a tiny little nation?"

My response dramatically changed the rest of the trip. I said, "Sir, the Bible says, in effect, that if God is not behind a military or government, the strength of its military will not give it victo—"

The man interrupted me with a loud stream of curse words. He veered to the shoulder, slammed on the brakes, and jammed his gearshift into "Park." Leaving the engine idling to run the air-conditioning, he screamed at me, at himself, and at God for the next 10 minutes.

"My private pilot is a Christian, my wife is a Christian, my children are born again Christians! It seems everybody that works for me these days is a Christian and I'm getting sick and tired of having Jesus thrown in my face! In fact, I am so sick of hearing about Jesus that I bought this car to drive from Connecticut to be alone and not have to listen to anyone—especially my pilot—talk about God!"

He continued, "When I saw your uniform, I knew a sailor wouldn't talk Jesus stuff." He pulled back onto the highway, and for next 250 miles, he chronicled his lifelong fight with and attempt to flee from God.

Then, spent and resigned, he turned to me and said, "Okay, I give up. Lead me in the prayer." He knew the prayer by heart but determined not to pray it with those who had harassed him about God for so many years.

We approached the throne together and he surrendered to our Lord and Savior. We had just crossed into South Carolina, and for the remainder of the trip, two brothers in the Lord rejoiced over his newfound freedom from sin, guilt, and shame.

He drove me to my parents' doorstep in Maitland, and we exchanged information. It turned out he was one of the highest-ranking executives in the Connecticut Mutual Life Insurance Company in Hartford. And the following week, he wrote me a nice term life policy!

CHAPTER 11

A Fragrance, an Odor, and a Fragrance

March 1974, Daytona Beach, Florida

W HO DOESN'T LOVE that new car smell? I first owned that glorious fragrance in 1974 when I bought a baby blue Volkswagen Karmann Ghia fresh off the showroom floor. On a Friday afternoon in March, after plunking down the $4,000 cash I had saved from my first two years in the Navy, I drove it straight from the Jacksonville dealership to my parents' house in Maitland. After a wonderful weekend, I headed back to my ship, docked in Mayport, 20 miles east of Jacksonville, committed to deeply inhaling all the way.

During my hitchhiking years, I had enjoyed a number of opportunities to share the Lord with each divinely appointed host who gave me a lift. Keeping my vow that I would repay those favors when I finally owned a car, I prayed for the Holy Spirit's guidance whenever I approached a hitchhiker. His permission followed no pattern that I could discern, and when I asked this time about a hippie sitting on his backpack and holding his thumb out just north of Daytona Beach, He clearly said, *"Yes, pick him up."*

As I pulled onto the shoulder and got a closer look, I quickly sought a second opinion from the Spirit to make sure He hadn't misspoken or I hadn't misheard. The hippie was a mountain of a man, sporting a bushy beard down to his breastbone and a ponytail halfway down his back, and wearing a tattered leather jacket that showed evidence of at least one knife fight. Everything about him indicated "tough guy."

Even before he got in the car, his unbathed fragrance preceded him and washed through the passenger compartment like a nauseating tidal wave. He threw his backpack onto the rear seat, shoehorned himself into the passenger's seat, and in a gruff baritone voice said, "I'm going to Jacksonville. I appreciate the lift."

As I quickly accelerated onto the highway, I saw him study the little plaque I had glued to my dashboard. It featured a well-known portrait of a smiling Jesus next to the words: *"If you meet me and forget me you've lost nothing. But if you meet Jesus Christ and forget him you've lost everything."*

My initial reaction was panic. How he might react? I mentally conjured an excuse to protect myself. I could tell him the car belonged to a friend who was one of those Jesus freaks. I didn't have time to polish that response before he turned to me and bellowed, "Are you a Christian?" My flesh demanded that I answer: "No!" But out of my mouth came a very calm and assured "Yes!"

As soon as I answered, he reached his right hand into his inside jacket pocket—much, I thought, as one would reach for a handgun. As he did so, I saw a satanic pentagram tattooed on his muscular forearm. I silently prayed: "Okay, Lord, I know why You wanted me to pick him up. It's my time to go home. Please give me the grace to die well."

But he pulled out of his jacket not a gun, but a little Gospel tract. "That's really weird," he said with a touch of confusion and fear. "Just 15 minutes before you picked me up this *really big* guy on a Harley stopped next to me and got off of his bike. I thought he was going to hurt me." He held up the tract. "But he pulled this out of his pocket, gave it to me, and kind of ordered me, 'Read this, it will save you.' Then he got on his bike and sped away.

"Before you picked me up, I read it through and thought, 'This is interesting, but I don't understand most of what I'm reading.'"

He followed up with the most beautiful question of the conversation, "Can you explain to me what this tract is talking about?" And for the next couple hours, I had the wonderful honor and privilege to introduce this giant of a man to his Savior.

I have wondered if God's angels stopped using chariots and are now using Harleys.

Alas, from that day forward I would never regain the new car smell of my precious little Ghia. During the two years I owned it, I tried many ways to mask the smell. Even Volkswagen dealerships couldn't restore that original aroma.

Eventually I stopped complaining about the big man's odor, and let it serve as a reminder that he no longer carried the stench of spiritual death. Instead, he will carry the aroma of Jesus Christ for all eternity.

CHAPTER 12

Learning from Broken Glass

1979, Olympic Peninsula of Washington State ...

D IANE: MICHAEL HAD JUST received a medical discharge from the Coast Guard, and wondered what the Lord wanted us to do next. His answer came in a challenge presented through a story we heard on the radio:

A widower had lovingly and caringly raised his two sons, but in his retirement, they found no time to visit him, even though they lived nearby in their small town. He had no transportation, and begged them incessantly by phone to stop by, but they were always too busy raising their own families, working, etc.

So the old man, knowing his sons, launched a brilliant plan. With the help of his friends and neighbors, he brought a flat-topped trunk from the basement into his dining room and filled with pieces of broken glass from windows, jars, bottles, and whatever else they could gather. He padlocked it and fastened a clear glass tabletop over it.

Then he phoned his sons and vowed that, if they would just come for Sunday dinner, he would never again pester them. They took the bait. As his boys sat at the new table, dad brought dinner from the kitchen and "accidentally" kicked the trunk. The glass reverberated like a treasure trove of coins. His sons' faces lit up. The father explained, "For many years now I have been cashing my savings and retirement checks and putting that money and my pocket change in the trunk for safekeeping."

For the next several years, his boys and their families brought dinner virtually every Sunday. When the father died, the sons held an elaborate funeral. Before the casket was buried, the sons were cutting the padlock on the trunk. When they opened it, Dad's ruse —and his lesson—became clear …

At this point, the radio storyteller asked, "Who or what did the sons really love—their father or what they would get from him?"

Our hearts broke over the implications of this story, as applied to our own love for God. Did Michael and I truly love Him for who He is? Or did we just love what we perceived He would give us now and in eternity? Did we really value Him? If all we ever received from our heavenly Father was a box of broken glass— would we love and serve Him from our hearts?

These questions caused us deep disquiet. We began a resolute search for biblical keys to walking with God on His terms, not ours. We fasted for two weeks (though we did feed the kids) and studied Job 1:9–11[17], and how God would have us live out Isaiah 61:1–11[18].

17. So Satan answered the Lord and said, "Does Job fear God for nothing? Have You not made a hedge around him, around his household, and around all that he has on every side? You have blessed the work of his hands, and his possessions have increased in the land. But now, stretch out Your hand and touch all that he has, and he will surely curse You to Your face!"

18. "The Spirit of the Lord God is upon Me,
Because the Lord has anointed Me
To preach good tidings to the poor;
He has sent Me to heal the brokenhearted,
To proclaim liberty to the captives,
And the opening of the prison to those who are bound;
To proclaim the acceptable year of the Lord,
And the day of vengeance of our God;
To comfort all who mourn,
 To console those who mourn in Zion,
To give them beauty for ashes,
The oil of joy for mourning,
The garment of praise for the spirit of heaviness;
That they may be called trees of righteousness,
The planting of the Lord, that He may be glorified.

"And they shall rebuild the old ruins,
They shall raise up the former desolations,
And they shall repair the ruined cities,
The desolations of many generations.
Strangers shall stand and feed your flocks,
And the sons of the foreigner
Shall be your plowmen and your vinedressers.
But you shall be named the priests of the Lord,
They shall call you the servants of our God.
You shall eat the riches of the Gentiles,
And in their glory you shall boast.
Instead of your shame you shall have double honor,
And instead of confusion they shall rejoice in their portion.
Therefore in their land they shall possess double;
Everlasting joy shall be theirs.

"For I, the Lord, love justice;
I hate robbery for burnt offering;
I will direct their work in truth,
And will make with them an everlasting covenant.
Their descendants shall be known among the Gentiles,
And their offspring among the people.

Over the next six months, we gave away nearly all of our possessions, paid off all our debts, and began an experiment in simplicity. God weaned us from materialism, from the expense and burden of superfluous things in the bondage of impressing others, and from the tyranny of seeking contentment or significance apart from knowing and doing His pleasure.

In 1996, when we moved into our tiny apartment in Siberia, we were very grateful for our years of learning a spare and simple lifestyle.

All who see them shall acknowledge them,
That they are the posterity whom the Lord has blessed.

"I will greatly rejoice in the Lord,
My soul shall be joyful in my God;
For He has clothed me with the garments of salvation,
He has covered me with the robe of righteousness,
As a bridegroom decks himself with ornaments,
And as a bride adorns herself with her jewels.
For as the earth brings forth its bud,
As the garden causes the things that are sown in it to spring forth,
So the Lord God will cause righteousness and praise to spring forth before all the nations."

CHAPTER 13

A Special Home Delivery

1980; on our 5th wedding anniversary in Joyce, Washington...

IANE: AT 8:32 SUNDAY MORNING, May 18, 1980, Mount St. Helens erupted just 138 miles southeast of us (as the ash flies). It shook our little family and tiny single-wide mobile home atop Mount Angeles in Joyce, Washington; population 382. Just 41 days later in the early hours of Saturday morning June 28th, another event rocked our little family.

Michael awakened our two eldest girls, Jeanne 4, and Becky just 24 days shy of her 3rd birthday to come into our tiny bedroom to watch the birth of our fourth child. Michael Jr. at 16 months was asleep in his crib nearby and remained undisturbed. Since our first three children had been birthed with no complications, we determined to have our fourth child naturally and at home. After all, for the first seven months of my pregnancy we prayed and reasoned that Michael had helped put the baby "in," God had given our baby life and with me nurtured our child in my womb—so why did we need to pay a doctor to catch our newborn?

With our Alexander Scourby Bible tapes playing in the background and the lights dimmed, daughter Bonnie came quietly into our family. She emerged gently into my husband's arms breathing with a slight whimper and no need for a thump on her rump. As Michael raised his sterilized scissors and stretched her tiny cord to sever it, Jeanne with elation in her voice nudged her younger sister and exclaimed, "LOOK, Becky, Daddy's cutting the baby's tail!"

When my labor began, Michael started playing the cassette at Psalm 1. As I cuddled Bonnie on my chest, Michael dabbed a cool damp cloth on my forehead, my two young girls softly probed their new sister, I closed my eyes and rested peacefully as a deep British voice read the 47th Psalm. We then exchanged tender congratulations, "Happy Anniversary, Sweetheart!"

CHAPTER 14

A Two-Wheeled Trip to Death's Door

July, 1980, Port Angeles, Washington

GOD HAS SPARED ME FROM death on many occasions. On His fourth time, He had to override my own folly to do so.

After my medical discharge from the Coast Guard, we moved from Joyce to Port Angeles and I enrolled at Peninsula College on the GI Bill to add general mechanics to my marine mechanics for foreign mission work. My 10-speed bike served as my transportation to and from school.

One evening at sunset, I left class just as an ominous thunderhead drifted over the mountain towards town. As I jumped on my Schwinn, a wall of rain pelted my back. I made an impetuous mental (mis)calculation, factoring in five known quantities that would help me outrun the rain—a 400-foot elevation drop down an arrow-straight first quarter mile of road; the stop sign at the ravine bridge, which I intended to snub; a steep mile-and-a-half downward grade after that; a sturdy bike with new tires powered by a buff ex-military 28-year-old body—and carelessly determined that I could outrace Mother Nature to my house.

The full-sized, four-door sedan was the one variable I had not considered.

The bike's speedometer pegged at 40 m.p.h. within the first few hundred yards. I was still accelerating about 50 feet from the bridge. I took one useless glance for cross traffic (houses and foliage formed blind spots on either side of the intersection) and streaked ahead.

I saw the car as I entered its path a few seconds before impact. I had no time to brake or avoid the collision. I barely had time to whisper, *"Father, I'm yours!"*

I saw, heard, and felt nothing as I bounced off the windshield and landed what the police determined to be 73 feet from the point of impact.

The driver, a Christian woman listening to worship songs as she drove up the mountain at 50 mph, veered on impact, and her right front wheel fork jammed onto a small concrete road marker, the only barrier that kept her from careening down the deep ravine. She later testified that she did not see me until my head slammed against her windshield and hurled her rear-view mirror into her rear window.

Ninety minutes later, the storm had passed and her car had been lifted back onto the road from its cliff side teeter. Safety crews had removed scraps of bicycle strewn across a 15-yard radius. A fire truck, two police cars, and an ambulance were on scene.

I "awoke," threw off the black tarp covering me, and sat up, dazed but oddly pain-free. I saw the coroner arrive and turned to see a police officer and two ambulance drivers about 15 feet away. They stopped their conversations and stared at me with dumbfounded incredulity. After an awkward silence, the officer, clearly shaken, pointed a trembling finger toward me, swallowed hard, and commanded, *"Lay down, you're dead!"* I didn't understand the significance of his comment, as I had no recollection of having arrived in heaven, hell, or purgatory.

I slowly and awkwardly rose to my feet. The three of them ran to me, steadied me, walked me to the ambulance, and rushed me to the hospital. During the ride, a pensive male voice spoke as though I could not hear: *"I don't believe this ... he was gone!"* At the hospital, the doctors examined me and declared that nothing was missing, broken, punctured, or dislocated.

After a police officer took me home that night, Diane fixed me a very hot Epsom salts bath. Over the next five weeks or so, I was covered head to ankles with ugly bruises and welts; I emerged from the experience with a greater appreciation for God's ability to protect His children from their most inane folly—because He has a future purpose to fulfill through them.

CHAPTER 15

"Quo Vadis?"[19]

August, 1980, Port Angeles, Washington

A FEW DAYS AFTER MY GRADUATION from Peninsula College, I told Diane that I sensed strongly in my
spirit that Father wanted me to hitchhike to Seattle that
week to hunt for a job. The busy ports of Seattle and Tacoma boast
many maritime companies and Navy shipyards that would likely
have employment suited to my particular skills and expertise.

I didn't know how long I would be gone, but I was certain this
was another God-adventure and that He would direct my ways
(Proverbs 3:5)[20]. She agreed, as she was confident our precious little church fellowship would help tend to her needs in my absence.

I stepped onto the highway at 6:00 a.m. Friday morning to
begin the 90-plus mile trip. I hitched three pleasant rides with
drivers who were open to the Gospel, and arrived in Seattle just
before noon. I started my search at the northernmost dock. At

19. Latin for "Where are you going?" or "Whither goest thou?"

20. Trust in the Lord with all your heart, and lean not on your own understanding.

the very first office, the receptionist responded to my DD-214 (official military veteran document) by giving me the address of the Washington State Employment Office where there worked a Veteran Liaison who would help me with finding vet-preferred job opportunities.

At 1:50 that afternoon, I sat in front of the liaison's desk, as he spoke by phone on my behalf with "George," the head disbursing officer aboard the U.S.S. *Fairweather*, a NOAA (National Oceanic and Atmospheric Administration) survey ship on Lake Union in Seattle. George asked to see me on the ship ASAP for an interview.

I arrived at 3:00. His only question: "Are you *really* an honorably discharged military veteran with GSA purchasing experience?" I showed him my documents, and he immediately responded with a big grin, "You're hired!" He then told me that the one other candidate was a shoo-in to be hired the next morning, but he was everything George loathed in a human being. So George was elated to give me the job.

He ended the meeting with the question, "How did you know I needed you here today?"

I told him, "I serve a God of divine appointments." George rolled his eyes. He wanted nothing to do with Jesus freaks, and he had just hired one!

A pair of return rides placed me back home in time for dinner, where I recounted my 12-hour adventure to my precious wife and we celebrated my new high-paying federal job as a U. S. Commerce Department purchasing agent with NOAA.

The following Monday morning, I reported to the ship for orientation and an induction physical. As I walked into the infirmary, the ship's head medical chief immediately recognized something about me. He read my name on my new personnel file and blurted, "This is not possible!" He continued, "You don't recognize me, do you, squid?"

Squid? I thought to myself, *how can he tell from the outside of my folder that I was in the Navy?* He answered my question, "You are the one and only Navy man I ever performed a discharge physical on at MacDill Air Force Base in Tampa, Florida. That was about late 1975, wasn't it?"

After some shared remembrances, punctuated with laughter and backslapping, he finished my medical checks. I went straight to my personal office on the ship, locked the door, got on my knees and wept, *"Wow, God, You did it again!"*

After five months of our working together, George had had about enough of my Jesus talk and let me know he was not impressed. We anchored at the small fishing village of Hoonah, Alaska, and George called me into his office. Following typical policy, he handed me the cash to purchase two months' of fresh groceries and other supplies for our crew of 200-plus men and women. I was to take members of the ship's food prep crew—they had the menu plans—and pay cash for all provisions. Scrawled at the top of the envelope was the figure "$12,000." Before I went ashore, I slipped into my office, counted the funds—and discovered that George had given me one $100 bill too many. I re-counted the money to confirm the error, and immediately went to George's office. I informed him of the oversight and handed him the bill.

George broke into tears, uttered a few obligatory curse words, and said with deep sorrow, "Michael, in the 20 years I've been doing this on two NOAA vessels, I have had to repay a lot of careless over-disbursements from my personal funds. Every one of my purchasers discovered my errors and pocketed the money with no way for me to prove the 'lost' cash. You really are serious about honoring Jesus, aren't you?"

"Yes, George," I told him. "He told me to honor you in all I do here, and that will honor Him."

I don't know whatever happened to George, but when I left NOAA to attend Bible College, I bought him a new Bible, which he gladly accepted.

CHAPTER 16

Holding My Daughter's Pain in My Hands

1982, my first semester at Philadelphia College of Bible ...

O NE AFTERNOON, AS I WAS DOING my homework, I heard a horrific shriek from our 6-year-old daughter, Jeanne. She ran into my office, screaming and holding her ear. She was so distraught and in pain she couldn't tell me what was wrong. I saw blood running down the side of her face and immediately rushed her to the hospital.

The emergency room technicians laid her on a table and asked me to hold her head still as a doctor examined her ear with a light scope. He quickly found the problem. The sharp point of a small artificial diamond was jammed against her eardrum. Apparently, Jeanne had found a faceted gem from a small child's ring. Wanting to look pretty for Daddy, she tried to press the pretty stone onto her earlobe as she ran to show me. Her pudgy little fingers slipped and she accidentally shoved the plastic diamond into her ear. In attempting to retrieve it, she pushed it in even further.

Now, wielding 12-inch long tweezers, the doctor was trying to perform a delicate cure on a confused and hysterical child who didn't understand that the several adults holding her down were only trying to help her.

The doctor indicated that he could not administer an anesthetic, and instructed me to hold Jeanne's head still while he extracted the danger. I firmly cupped her face in my hands and looked into her eyes. She glared back at me through tears and screamed, "Daddy, why are you letting this man hurt me!?"

How could I explain to my precious 6-year-old that letting this stranger hurt her was the most loving and compassionate thing I could do? She hadn't done anything wrong; she just wanted to please her Daddy. Yet I had to allow her to be hurt to prevent a greater evil from befalling her.

That incident often came to mind over the years as I found myself in a position or circumstance where enemies were maliciously causing me pain, even as I innocently sought to please my Heavenly Father. I would cry out, "Daddy, why are you letting this person hurt me?"

Now I know His answer: *"I have to—for now. But it'll all be better."*[21]

---

21. 2 Corinthians 1:3-5

CHAPTER 17

Fed by the Mafia

1982, my second semester at Philadelphia College of Bible ...

W E WERE ASKED TO MOVE (rent-free) into and temporarily operate Grace Settlement House, an evangelistic outreach to an Italian Catholic neighborhood, blocks from the infamous Italian Market near the center of Philadelphia.

As a family we reached out daily to the 'hood in Jesus' name. I focused on the practical needs of several elderly widows on the block and ministered to several—ahem—"local independent curbside pharmaceutical merchants." Diane and our children focused on the neighborhood kids, most of whom lived in very disheartening circumstances both on the streets and at home.

Those kids came to us daily to receive a variety of services, including dinner at our table, clothing, overnight shelter, Bible study, Sunday morning services, and help with schoolwork.

Within a few blocks of the home were several pizza parlors. As one particular pizza restaurant owner became familiar with us, our outreach, our children, and our finances, he started fixing two of his largest "everything" pizzas daily at 5:00 p.m., and graciously charged us a total of only $5 for both pies.

That is, until he learned through the grapevine that we had hurting and homeless children coming to our evening table each day.

One afternoon, about an hour before we were to go pick up our daily pizzas, a delivery boy from the restaurant delivered four large pizzas, two bags of hot breadsticks, and a couple bags of boxed spaghetti. He had been instructed to tell us that there had been a "cancelled party order" and they'd rather us use the food than throw it away.

Later that week, I approached the owner to thank him for his gift. He assured me, "I wanna help you help the kids in the 'hood." He said the restaurant wasn't there to sell pizza. "It's a *family* business." His inflection and wink of an eye implied a particular import of the word "family." My blank look solicited a more direct hint, so he explained that his "family assets" needed to be "cleaned" through "legitimate business accounts." *Aah, now I get it.*

Directed by the hand of God, that piping hot manna continued daily in the quantity appropriate to our daily need until we moved out of the inner city.

CHAPTER 18

A Cup of Gasoline

Summer 1983, Camp Iroquoina,
Hallstead, Pennsylvania ...

W E LIVED AT A CHRISTIAN camp the summer
before my senior year of Bible college. In exchange
for rent, I was asked to repair and maintain the
groundskeeping equipment, help with building projects, and as-
sist camp staff with counseling and oversight.

As Daddy's girl, daughter Jeanne was always eager to help me in
whatever I was doing. One morning, as I rebuilt a camp lawnmow-
er's carburetor, I needed a small cup of gasoline from the maintenance shed. Seven-year-old Jeanne came out and asked if she could
help. I trusted she could handle a five-gallon gas can and find an
appropriate container among many small coffee cans nearby. So I
said, "Yes, honey, I need a cup of gasoline."

She cheerfully skittered off toward the shed. After about 10
minutes, I thought she perhaps had forgotten my instructions or
had gotten sidetracked. So I headed to the maintenance shed to
check on her.

As I rounded the corner and looked inside, I saw Jeanne, utterly bewildered, standing near a sizable pool of gasoline. All around her feet were the steadily dissolving remains of perhaps a dozen Styrofoam cups. Her cheeks tear stained, she held one such melted ring in her hand. Uncompromising chemical forces far beyond her understanding had defeated her sincerest repeated attempts to please her Daddy.

As I scooped her in my arms and assured her she was not at fault and I was not disappointed with her, I tried not to envision the trauma Jeanne had endured as her joyful efforts to please me turned to confusion, then to frustration, and finally to helplessness with every new attempt to bring me the cup of gasoline I had requested.

The experience did offer an object lesson that evening, however. I told Jeanne that certain containers simply cannot hold certain liquids. It's the same with our minds and bodies. We were created to be vessels of His Spirit for His glory and honor and we need to avoid the many spiritual, physical, and emotional poisons that inhibit or destroy our ability to be God's available and usable vessels.

CHAPTER 19

A Barehanded Divine Appointment

Spring 1985

FOR MANY YEARS, WHILE OUR children were growing up, I played in city, church, and military softball leagues. And, just in case an opportunity for an impromptu game arose, I kept my mitt, a couple softballs, and my favorite bat in my car trunk.

One afternoon, as I was out job hunting, I drove by a local church not far from our home, and saw a softball game in progress. I pulled behind the backstop, opened the trunk for my gear, and asked if they needed a pitcher. The team on the field invited me to take the mound. The other lefty on the team played right field, so I loaned him my glove and pitched with no mitt. In the third inning, with a runner on first and no outs, a very large collegiate athlete with forearms thicker than my calves stepped up to the plate.

The man smashed a line drive that whistled about three feet to my left. I instinctively reached out, and in one motion, caught the ball barehanded and whipped it to the first baseman, nipping the runner off first for a double play.

The first baseman underhanded the ball back to me, and as I prepared for the next pitch, I felt my hand throbbing. As I toed the rubber, our shortstop shouted, "Look at the ball!" I looked down to see that the ball was completely red and dripping with blood. Curious and not immediately comprehending the situation, I lifted and turned my hand and noted that my pinky finger was dangling by a narrow bridge of skin and muscle, with the bone exposed.

My first thought was, *"Oh, no! Diane thinks I am looking for a job and I've just incurred a huge medical debt we can't afford."*

I dropped the ball to more closely examine my injury. As I did so, one of my outfielders ran up, grabbed my wrist to inspect, and assured me that he could help. Noting the suspicious look on my face, he continued, "Are you familiar with the dental office down the street?"

I retorted in jest, "This isn't filling a cavity!"

He laughed and with a reassuring smile said, "Yes, I'm a dentist, but in Vietnam I was a front-line field surgeon and patched up lots of nasty hand and foot wounds. Come on down to my office and we'll fix this up."

He was also a born again Christian, and for the next three hours, I sat in one of his dental chairs as he delicately repaired my hand and spoke of his love for Christ. I told him of my life, family, ministry, and dream to someday go to the foreign mission field.

Several weeks later, he removed the stitches, I bought him lunch, and he considered the surgery paid in full.

CHAPTER 20

Fighting the War on the Right Front

1988, Kensington neighborhood in Philadelphia ...

I T WAS MOVE-IN DAY. My 12-year-old daughter, Becky, and I were hauling boxes from our VW van into our just purchased row home in a tough, run-down, inner city neighborhood where I would spend the next four years reaching out to the night people.

Our front door opened to a two-acre park where children and pets frolicked and the elderly warmed a dozen or more benches by day, and crack cocaine was king after sundown. Our real estate agent warned that our first day would not pass without an official visit from the feared drug lord who "owned" our contiguous four square block turf.

As promised, he and a bodyguard thusly "welcomed" us to the 'hood: As Becky, laden with another box, approached our front door, she was intercepted by the two menacing figures. As he stiff-armed Becky's box, the dealer addressed her but aimed his intimidating glare and implicit challenge at me, "Hi, little sweetie, you give me all the sex I want, and I'll give you all the drugs and goodies you want!" With that, he took an offensive stance to await my reaction and began boasting of his little kingdom.

His voice quickly faded as my mind formulated a strategy. Motivated by fleshly anger and seeking a worldly solution, I envisioned how things would play out: *The hospital down the street housed many worthy souls desperately needing organ donations. With my special and lethal Navy and Coast Guard training, I could swiftly remove several organs from their worthless carcasses before they breathed their last.* Then I implored God's rubber stamp approval: *"Please, God, can I? Can I, please?!"*

When my nemesis finished, I smiled kindly and graciously escorted Becky toward the house. I telegraphed no malice, but every fiber within me was taut and wary, ready to repel their attack and vanquish them in hand-to-hand combat. I had just turned my back on them and—

WHAM!

I reeled from the impact.

No, neither member of our personal welcoming committee had touched me. It was the Holy Spirit who slapped me upside my head with the harshest rebuke I had ever received from Him: *I put you here because I want to save those young men's souls!*[22] *I don't want you fighting against them; I want you fighting for them! You are to wage spiritual warfare—the battle they cannot fight—on their behalf!*[23]

Beginning that night, I daily knelt in intercession for those young men.

One early evening during my second year of praying for them, I answered a knock at the front door. There stood the dealer,

22. Matthew 18:21–35

23. 2 Corinthians 4:3–5

trembling and sobbing, tears cascading down his face. He blubbered out a barely intelligible plea for me to come to his house and pray for his beloved mother, who was dying of a cancer all his drug money and thuggish bravado could not heal. That night, at her bedside, he gave his life to Jesus. He later moved to live with a grandmother in another state, and the last I heard—14 years ago—he was working full-time in the Gospel ministry.

CHAPTER 21

The Church v. the Pregnant Lady

1989, Philadelphia ...

SUNDAY MORNING SERVICE AT THE small Bible church we attended during our street ministry in Philadelphia went, well, normally. We were just about to launch into the last verse of "Oh, How I Love Jesus" to end the service when the Lord indelibly tested that pronouncement.

"I'm single, my married boss got me pregnant, mom kicked me out, and if I don't get help I'm going to abort my baby tomorrow morning!" blared the thirty-something woman from just inside the back entrance of the church.

As her rude interruption reverberated through the sanctuary, the entire congregation turned in unison and stared at the intruder. Some parishioners were, no doubt, momentarily trying to sort out the implications of the unusual disruption. Others expressed significant annoyance. And far too many shot her a look of self-righteous contempt.

The pastor quickly rebuked her for contaminating our Christian worship with her sin, and barked the order that she leave at once.

I didn't at all mind her interruption, but I was profoundly offended at the fellowship's response to her. Diane and I looked at each other and instantly made a silent pact. I left my pew, hustled over to her, and put my arm around her shoulder. I whispered that we were going to take her into our home and care for her until her child was born.

Though the next seven months were extremely difficult for us, financially and logistically, our efforts were well rewarded when her mother visited the hospital when her granddaughter was born and tearfully told her daughter, "If strangers can forgive you, take you in, and love you, then I can, too." From that day on, she cared for her daughter and her precious newborn, who, as of this writing, is 26 years old!

CHAPTER 22

My Son, My Hero

1993, Lake Mary, Florida ...

I HAVE FEW HEROES—dead or alive—in my life. But one inhabitant of that sparsely populated pantheon is my son Michael Jr.

He was a lanky five-foot-ten-inch 15 year old when he earned that title. One afternoon I drove to a high school football field in Lake Mary, Florida to pick him up after a pick-up game of unprotected tackle football. I arrived early, parked the car, jumped onto the hood, and watched the game's final half hour. Surveying the gladiators, I noticed that Michael was among the youngest, least muscular, and most inexperienced participants in the battle.

I watched as Michael caught a kickoff and sprinted his fastest downfield. He'd gone about 20 yards at full rip when two very big and very powerful opponents simultaneously hit him with a force that made my teeth rattle. Unimpeded, they slammed him to the ground, both of them landing on top of him. After a few elbow jabs and knee shots, they rolled off him and jive-trotted away.

I honestly expected Michael's next physical movement to require the assistance of EMTs, but to everyone's amazement—including mine—my son jumped up, shot a look of undiluted defiant contempt at his tacklers, strutted to his huddle, and played with undiminished passion and skill the remainder of the game.

That night, I asked him about the hit. Did it hurt?

"Dad, it felt like every muscle and bone in my body was bruised," he told me. "But I was not about to let them think they had hurt me!"

Many times since then a circumstance, or people, or my own stupidity or ignorance has knocked me so flat I thought I'd never get up again. But then the Holy Spirit would remind me of that hit Michael took so valiantly—so heroically. And I have learned that, with God's power and strength, I can do the same.

CHAPTER 23

On a Wing and a Prayer (Part 1)

September-October 1994, first trip to Siberia via England and Moscow ...

WHENEVER I TRAVEL, I ASK Father for divine appointments—and I have learned to expect them. But I've never been so blessedly inundated with His miraculous arrangements than during my first trip to Siberia two years before we were to move there.

If all went as planned, I would board the plane in Florida, land in Manchester, England, take the railway to London where I would stay overnight, take the next morning's flight to Kiev, Ukraine for a two-week mission stay, then end up with a two-week mission trip to Moscow.

And everything *did go* as planned ... until just before I boarded the plane in Florida.

Just before I got on the plane, I called the team leader I was to meet in London. He said another team member could not get his documents; therefore, our Ukraine trip was abruptly cancelled. Thus I faced two weeks in Manchester, England with no provision and no place to stay.

I didn't doubt I was beginning a God-trip, having seen the miraculous ways God had brought in the funding—all unsolicited, and all precisely on time. So I knew my God had a plan, and He would give me a ringside seat from which to watch it unfold ...

I settled into my window seat and touched the empty seats to my left, praying for my anticipated appointments. Soon a British man sat by me; his wife took the aisle seat. He initiated a conversation by asking about my occupation. I responded that I was a Christian minister focused at that time on helping young people trapped in drug abuse. I added that God can break any addiction. The wife began to cry, quickly excused herself, and ran to the lavatory.

The man explained that they had flown to the U.S. to escape a bad problem at home and to discuss their divorce. Their only son's out-of-control drug addiction was destroying their marriage and their lives. For most of our transatlantic flight we spoke about their son's troubles and our ministry. Shortly before we landed, they asked me about my stay in England. I relayed my predicament: two weeks stranded in Manchester with nowhere to lodge and no financial resource for food, drink, or shelter.

After a brief hushed confab, they offered a proposal. They owned a bed and breakfast in a small village near Manchester. They would take care of all my needs if I would work with their son.

It was a wonderful two weeks. I counseled their son and ministered the Word to the entire family—and their employees, neighbors, and pub mates; in return, I was pampered at a classy British B&B. My hosts also purchased my roundtrip train tickets to London.

Everyone involved was blessed beyond measure. But, then again, that was God's plan after all.

* * * * * *

When I arrived in London another "surprise" itinerary change awaited me.

We had been asked to make a seven-day 3,000-mile round trip to Novosibirsk in south-central Siberia. The trip would cost just under a thousand dollars. I had no funds and only that night to decide. The team and I stayed in the home of a London pastor who let me call Diane in Florida to pray together about the new itinerary.

Diane giggled and told me that a large gift earmarked for my trip had come in too late to apply to my expenses thus far. That tardy gift was—almost to the dollar—the amount I needed for the round trip to Novosibirsk and some discretionary funds too! Within 24 hours, Diane wired those funds, and we received the money in time to purchase the tickets.

* * * * * *

When I stepped onto the tarmac at the Novosibirsk airport, I was overcome by a sense of home unlike any quickening I had ever received—an unshakable conviction that Diane and I were being called to Siberia.

About 15 minutes later I received my first personal welcome. A young boy left his father's side and ran to me, stopped about two feet away, spat on my favorite cowboy boots, and viciously growled, "American, I hate you!" I just smiled at him and walked away.

I had long before developed the habit (during my travels to 33 countries around the globe) of walking solo in whatever city I entered to explore and find locals with whom I could share Father's love. My first morning in Novosibirsk, armed with an English-Russian pocket dictionary, I set out to explore the city.

After about three hours, I "stumbled" onto the campus of Novosibirsk State University. I purchased black bread, caviar, and a bottle of water and sat on the campus lawn to eat lunch and contemplate. If Father was calling us to Siberia, I would need a right arm and a crack translator, a keen young man to walk with us. I knelt and prayed for the young man I sensed was there on campus. I prayed for his present and future needs and that Father would bring him to Himself and to me.

* * * * * *

Three weeks later, I entered our rolling home back in Longwood, Florida, and before I could speak, Diane gleefully chirped, "We're going to Siberia, aren't we?!" I never asked her to go anywhere that Father had not called her, too. We still had two children in high school, so then was not the time to move overseas. We agreed that our kids were our first priority—our first mission field—and we waited on Father's timing.

CHAPTER 24

On a Wing and a Prayer (Part 2)

Yakutsk, 1998 ...

BEFORE FATHER GIFTED US WITH a ministry helper, we used unsaved translators whenever possible so the Holy Spirit could convert their souls as they converted our English into Russian and Sakhali.

For seven months, I was blessed with a talented translator for the largest evangelical church in Yakutsk, which met at the Maritime River College. He was so proficient; I could cover a lot of information in a one-to-three hour sermon with few breaks.

At the beginning of the eighth month of my preaching stint, I preached the sermon I am most known for in America: an inductive study of Luke 13:6–9[24], the parable of the unfruitful fig tree.[25]

---

24. He also spoke this parable: "A certain man had a fig tree planted in his vineyard, and he came seeking fruit on it and found none. Then he said to the keeper of his vineyard, 'Look, for three years I have come seeking fruit on this fig tree and find none. Cut it down; why does it use up the ground?' But he answered and said to him, 'Sir, let it alone this year also, until I dig around it and fertilize it. And if it bears fruit, well. But if not, after that you can cut it down.'"

25. In fact, I am known in many places as "The Poopie Pastor."

Over the course of that two-hour sermon, I developed the concept of God using stinky, uncomfortable circumstances in our lives to grow tasty eternal fruit. I asked the audience to think back in their lives to places where fertilizer was applied. "When we think of dung[26] or fertilizer," I asked, "which of the five senses is most stimulated? Obviously, our sense of smell."

"How many times," I continued, "have we deeply resented a situation and said to our Heavenly Father, 'God, this situation really *stinks*'? Well, instead of automatically rebuking the devil or thinking God doesn't like us, perhaps we should consider that He is fertilizing us. When we see that it is a loving God who is fertilizing, we will be more apt to trust and give ourselves to Him."

When I had communicated that point in the sermon, my translator went silent for almost a full minute. I turned to see if he had misunderstood and repeated the statement. We finished the service and agreed to meet for Monday lunch. During our walk to the restaurant, he reminded me of the pause during my fertilizer punch line.

"Yes," I responded. "I wondered what it was you didn't understand."

"It was not a translation problem," he said. "It was a heart problem."

He explained that, at that moment, he was doing business with God over some nasty fertilizer in his life. "During that pause, I was giving my life to the Lord!"

Amen! At that point he became my right arm in Siberia.

He told me a most remarkable story about a "fertilizer affliction" that kept him angry at God for four years. In October 1994, he was a student at the Novosibirsk State University. At the mention of the university, I was all ears. The chair of his academic department (such administrators were under no obligation to graduate any student, regardless of their academic standing) told

---

26. King James Version

my helper that he was not allowing him to graduate because of a (mistakenly) perceived personal offense.

My helper was forced to find another university to finish his studies—and the only available option was to attend Yakutsk State University, nearly 3,000 miles to the northeast. After graduation, he stayed, met and married his precious wife, and made their home in Yakutsk.

For my part in our unlikely union, God sent me 6,600 miles four years earlier to that very campus—only days before he sat in the department head's office getting the boot—to intercede for the man He had ordained to help in our ministry.

CHAPTER 25

Fish Heads and Eyeballs

Fall 1996, at our first Sakha
family picnic ...

D IANE: I WAS ALWAYS TAUGHT to be a gracious guest and eat what was put in front of me. But this?! Really?!

Before we had left for Russia, Michael and I made the commitment to adopt the customs and practices of the native peoples we were called to serve. That meant getting used to some strange and often inconvenient ways, including eating the local cuisine, but we determined to live out the well-known precept: "Where He leads me I will follow; what He feeds me I will swallow." Our doing so bolstered our standing in the community and endeared us to the wonderful people of the Sakha Republic.

Our first autumn in Siberia, we were invited to a picnic at the family home of one of our students. They were very generous and hospitable, and we felt so privileged that the Lord called us there to pour our lives into those students. We loved the students, and their families reciprocated that affection to us. With few exceptions, every student's home was open to us.

The picnic began with some guttural singing, similar to Native American chants, by a shaman to honor all those who attended the gathering. After his song, we proceeded to the long hand-hewn picnic table. I noted the sumptuous variety of food: several species of fish, different kinds of bread topped with sour cream and fruit preserves, salted cabbage and carrots, frozen raw horsemeat cubes for dessert, and fermented mare's milk to wash it all down.

But the gastronomic centerpiece of the event was *karasee* (pronounced "KAH-rah-see," with a slight roll of the "r" and the emphasis on the first syllable), a favorite of the Sakha people. Karasee is a river fish, about five to seven inches long. On that day they were impaled vertically on wooden spikes anchored at regular intervals along the middle of the table.

An elderly Sakha grandmother sat on a hand-carved bench at the table between Michael and me. She smiled, nodded at me, and motioned for me to follow her example. She then slid one of the fish off its spike, took it in both hands, split the head from front to back in one smooth motion—and with one hearty slurp, sucked out the brains and eyes!

She gestured for me to try the delicacy in the same manner. I had closely watched her, so I was ready for my turn—at least in technique. I took a fish, placed my fingers between the gills and eyes, and ripped it open. I sucked out the brains and eyes, and for a moment, could not believe what my taste buds were telling me. I turned to the grandmother and beamed, "*Na-ha minye-gas!*" (Sakhali for "Very delicious!")

Well, Michael was not going to be outdone by a couple of women. So he repeated the procedure with a karasee, and also confirmed it to be: "Delicious!"

That experience immediately endeared us to that Sakha family. So many foreigners and visitors had refused to eat their cuisine, disparaging the food as disgusting or unworthy. But God granted us a gracious, gentle miracle in disconnecting our eye gates from our gag reflexes during that first fish head meal, and we not only learned a new, practical way to honor the Sakha people, but enjoyed a savory new taste as a bonus.

CHAPTER 26

God's (Literally) Warm Embrace

Fall 1996, Yakutsk Polytechnical College, Yakutsk ...

L ongwood, Florida to northern Siberia is a long trip ... in many ways.

One of those distances is meteorological. Temperatures which rarely crack 50° F during winter nights in central Florida routinely dip below -60° F for weeks on end just below the Arctic Circle.

Such diametric weather extremes can kill someone who is not adequately prepared. It is imperative to gradually acclimate to the frigid temperatures and wear the appropriate winter garb to survive. Fur and felt are the materials of choice, as manmade materials disintegrate in such a constantly brutal climate.

We first arrived in Siberia during the fall of 1996. We were hired on by a state-run college where we taught English, making far below the U. S. minimum wage and receiving no financial support from the States. Each passing day saw another drop in temperature, ratifying the daily observations of the locals of an impending terribly cold winter, and ratcheting up our friends' desperate pleas for us to be sensible and head back to the safety of a less lethal climate.

The need for sufficient winter outerwear nagged at Diane's and my thoughts, but we were without means to afford the necessary protection. One of Diane's younger brothers had been a furrier, so she knew of both the utility and expense of a fur coat. Fur prices in Russia were a bit lower than those in America, but even the reduced cost was far beyond our reach. Nevertheless, every time Diane saw a gorgeous fur coat (among the most beautiful we had ever seen) in a store or on other women, she verbalized her own need for one. Her comments were accompanied by almost tangible visions of her tightly snuggled into the glorious soft warmth of the garment she longed for.

Each time she mentioned the need, however, our Russian and Sakha friends waved off her spoken desire, and encouraged her to resist the purchase. I, prompted by the soft voice of the Holy Spirit, gently concurred.

The first morning the temperature dipped below the freezing mark, a girl from another class crept into Diane's classroom, and to the amused titters of students, approached her from behind, surreptitiously and strategically measured her dimensions, and quickly scampered out of the room. Diane was rather annoyed at the distraction, but quickly returned her attention to her classroom duties and gave it no further thought.

A few days later, the college president, with an entourage of VIPs, joyfully invaded Diane's morning class and, with some considerable fanfare, awarded her a breathtakingly elegant—and expensive—full-length fur coat of 4-inch thick exotic lambs' wool.

Half an hour later, with much less ado, a gentleman entered my classroom and presented me with a brand new men's winter coat.

The outside consisted of a heavily stitched waterproof black canvas. The coat was lined with the pelts of five full-grown golden retrievers.

We sported those wonderful gifts with immense gratitude through several winters.

CHAPTER 27

A Rescue at Fifty Below

1997, north central Siberia ...

O N THE SAKHA MISSION FIELD, we asked God to make our decisions for us, as we knew that any direction Diane or I took according to our flesh or human wisdom could quickly destroy us. Insensitivity to the Spirit's leading carries a razor thin margin of error in the treacherous conditions of northern Siberia.

In the early winter of 1997, two small U.S. churches donated enough money for us to purchase a new four-wheel-drive Russian YAZ ("*Oo-aaz*") van. We took possession of the vehicle just in time to "enjoy" the region's perilous travel conditions during the annual change to winter.

A Sakha friend and I christened the van with an adventurous maiden voyage: a four- to six-day 480-mile trip along untested, shifting terrain to an isolated needy village north of Vilyuysk. The van was stuffed with more than 650 pounds of food staples, medical supplies, and three 55-gallon drums of gasoline.

The temperatures had been hovering at about -50° F for a week, but the ground was not fully hardened. Everyone counseled us to forgo the trip until more fortuitous weather settled in. I prayed diligently for God's wisdom and perceived Father's pleasure to go. My friend, raised in the taiga, agreed to drive, impelled by the prospect of helping a village of his people survive the coming winter.

We covered about 130 miles in the first 30 hours. Then, without warning, about 3:00 a.m., our little water cooled 4-cylinder engine died. My friend tried every trick he knew to restart it, but it would not come back to life. With the temperature at -50° F, we had less than 20 minutes to restart the engine with warm oil and gasoline, or our lifeless bodies would not be found until spring.

My friend jumped out of the van and slipped his slender body between the undercarriage and the snow. He discovered that, just before the engine died, the main radiator hose from the engine block had been dislodged and all the radiator fluid had drained out. Miraculously, the hose was not missing or damaged, and the metal clamp was still attached, dangling on the end of the hose. He quickly reconnected and secured the hose with tools from his little kit.

The radiator was mounted inside the passenger compartment between the two front seats to help keep it and the passengers from freezing during winter operation. We quickly poured our last two 1.5-liter bottles of home mixed Russian "Kool-Aid" into the radiator, and then we took turns urinating into it. The reservoir was half full when we closed the cap and turned to our only Hope.

We clasped hands and laid our free hands on the engine as if it were an ailing relative. My friend did not speak English, and I knew little Russian or Sakhali. We had no translator, so most of our communication was by eye contact, charades, hand gestures, and head movement. I have never forgotten my loud petition that morning:

"LORD, You did not bring us into this remote wilderness to kill us and allow these supplies You provided to be stranded away from

their destination. You created every molecule in Your universe and You keep them by Your mighty wisdom and power. I simply ask, Father, that You heal our inanimate engine and get us safely to the destination You ordained for this time. Amen!"

My friend was then unsaved and clueless to what I had said, but he did recognize the "amen" and loudly echoed the Russian version: "A-MEEN!"

With scant minutes to spare, he turned the key—and the engine immediately came to life. About six hours later we reached a tiny village where one of the residents played the role of guardian angel to two improbable strangers. He provided us with food, drink, and bed rest, and allowed us to park our van in his attached heated garage, where we flushed and refilled the radiator and made several other minor repairs and adjustments.

We finished the trek, delivered the much needed supplies to a very appreciative gathering of villagers, and returned home safely, all under the watchful eye and gentle hand of a sovereign, miracle working God who knows how to fulfill His purposes, despite the greatest obstacles.

CHAPTER 28

Classrooms of Prizewinners

1997–1998, throughout the Sakha Republic ...

SHORTLY AFTER ARRIVING IN SIBERIA, we presented ourselves as willing servants to the governmental authorities in Yakutsk, the capital city of the Sakha Republic. "However you need us," we promised, "we are available to you and your people, no matter what."

Little did we know how far-flung the people in need were and how impassable the access to them. We had neither the transportation nor the means to reach all those towns and villages. In our 11 years there, we only reached 62 of the republic's 529 communities, and even that taxed our strength, time, and resources to the limit.

Enter God—and His sovereign provision.

In 1997, English was declared to be the republic's third official language to equip the next generation in global computer and business literacy. The President authorized the Ministry of Education to launch Intensus Language Schools throughout the republic. When Intensus opened in the capital, only two native English speakers/available teachers lived there: Diane and I.

Every Friday across the republic, towns and villages held linguistic contests as the best English students paraded their skills. Each week's winners won a government funded trip to the capital for a week of intensive study in conversational English under the tutelage of native speakers. So, every week our classrooms were filled with the best and brightest future leaders from every corner of the republic—and Diane and I were free to converse about whatever we wanted, without interference or censorship ...

So, our sovereign Father let His message be spread throughout the republic without cost to His messengers or to its recipients. Most of those students are now in their 30s and 40s in important positions throughout the Sakha Republic.

CHAPTER 29

My Favorite Wife

1996, Yakutsk ...

ONE OF RUSSIA'S SPECIAL ANNUAL holidays is called International Women's Day, and our first year there, Diane was invited to a large Women's Day celebration.

My job was to pick her up after the banquet, but unfortunately I got the time mixed up and arrived 40 minutes early. I was surprised that the ladies in the room were glad to see me and invited me to join Diane at the VIP table, because men are not allowed at such banquets unless they are serving and cleaning tables.

Obligatory toasts are given early in the celebration, but I was nevertheless invited later on to offer an official toast as well. Without hesitation, I stood up, grabbed my wine glass, lifted it high and waited for the women to follow suit, and declared with a twinkle in my eye, "To women, the best thing that ever happened to a rib!" I was stunned when the entire room erupted in laughter. Diane and I looked at each other in shock; we had anticipated that perhaps only a handful of women knew anything about Adam and Eve.

We later discovered that, throughout the Soviet era, the Russians had learned most of the same Genesis stories we in America learned in Sunday school. In fact, Bible stories in Russia are considered on the same level as Grimms' Fairy Tales and Aesop's fables to American children.

Immediately after my "rib" toast, I asked the MC if I could toast Diane. Upon receiving permission, I opened with a remark I often gave at weddings officiated or attended: "This lady sitting next to me is my favorite wife." Everyone there knew Diane was my *only* wife, and their looks of puzzlement signaled they needed further explanation.

So I mischievously continued: "True, I've only been married to one woman, but I have slept with 26 different women." I knew this might incite a sterner reaction, but since Diane did not visibly react badly to that statement, the ladies perceived there was a deeper meaning.

"You see," I said, "26 years ago I married a beautiful, slender, dark-haired recent college graduate and beauty queen. A year later I was married to a mother of one who had put on a few extra pounds. Over each of the next 25 years, my Diane changed, becoming a different person, until she's the same—but different— beautiful woman you see today. And every year, I choose to fall in love with the woman I am married to then, and not hang on to the person or personality I was married to the year before."

They got it!

CHAPTER 30

"Call on Me"

1998, Vilyuysk ...

WHEN I TOLD A HIGH-RANKING Russian official friend that we were moving to the most perilous and closed region of his republic, he cautioned me that I would probably have much difficulty with government types. He sternly warned me not to defend myself or deal with such difficulties in my own way. He said, "I have great authority and influence, and you are to call on me when you have need."

It didn't take long for that need to arrive.

Two weeks after we moved to Vilyuysk, I was required to make an important registration with a local government official. My request was unaccompanied by an appropriate bribe, which angered and offended him. He leaned back in his chair and said with a sneer, "I'm going on a hunting trip for two weeks—starting in 30 minutes—and your limit is one week to have this registration stamped. I am not going to fulfill your request and I'll make sure you are fined for your delay." My translator assured me that arguing with this man could get me a severe beating or jail time.

I asked the official if I could use the phone in his office, but did not tell him whom I was calling. When I explained my circumstances to my high-ranking friend, he said, "Please hand the phone to the official." I did not understand the conversation, but the official became unnerved. He hung up the phone and within 10 minutes he had taken care of my documentation.

The One who watches over me as I travel throughout the world has said in His Word, *"All authority has been given to Me in heaven and on earth. Go therefore ..."* Far too often I have tried to fix problems myself and made a worse mess. But when I rely on the Sovereign One, He always moves the hearts of those who stand in the way of what He wants me to do.

CHAPTER 31

Defeating the Enemy with a Load of Fish

1999, Vilyuysk ...

I N RUSSIA, NOT ALL "CHRISTIANS" are created equal—
and very few sects are welcome.

Centuries of well-meaning but inartful missionary attempts
to convert the locals to a brand of religion both irrelevant to their
lives and powerless to comfort and heal their deepest needs , had
given rise to the consensus that "religion only brings trouble."

Into that pool of communal skepticism Diane and I waded—
neck deep.

Shortly after we moved into our new home in Vilyuysk in 1998,
we were visited by emissaries from the surrounding towns and
villages; nearly all of them warned us that we were never to set
foot among them or we would suffer the unarticulated but un-
questionably malevolent consequences.

In issuing these threats, however, they challenged not us, but
God.

After receiving such an ultimatum from a delegation from the village directly across the river, I repeated an oft-spoken prayer: *"Lord, do in and among these people whatever You have to do, whatever it takes to have Your way in them. And, if You so please, use us in that process."* I then added that village to my daily prayer list.

Barely a year after that initial threat, God got the next word, and we, in obedience to Him, made the next move.

It was a bitterly cold winter night when we received the terrible news. A woman in the village across the river had suffered a horrible accident and died, leaving behind an invalid husband and nine children. One of her youngest children found her frozen to death in their back yard.

Upon hearing the news, the hunter/fisherman who lived with us and I backed our four-wheel-drive van up to our cold storage shed, in which we had stored winter provisions for our family and several other families we regularly helped feed. We covered the entire floor of the van with several dozen of our biggest pike, salmon, and other large river fish. We also loaded other staples (flour, beans, etc.) into the vehicle and collected what few rubles we had left.

During the late evening hours, we cautiously drove across the frozen river, snuck through a back entrance to the village, and drove to the grieving family's house. The woman's body was lying on her bed. Her husband sat silent and despondent in the living room. The children all shared the grief of loss, and each exhibited their own unique combination of anger, anguish, and fear.

We spent a couple hours ministering to the family as we could, and helped prepare her body for the burial. We presented each child with a glossy children's picture Bible in the Sakha language.

Finally, we and the children formed a brigade to unload the fish from the van onto their back porch, where the food would stay frozen until needed.

A few days later, that same village delegation returned to our door. Their spokesperson said, humbly and simply, "You are welcome in our village. We did not realize that yours was a religion of love."

CHAPTER 32

God Only Needs Your Mouth

1999, a remote village in the Sakha Republic ...

I T WAS A SCHEDULE OFTEN repeated during our church-planting endeavors in Siberia:

6:00 A.M.

After a nine-hour drive through the wilderness, we arrive in the remote village of just under 500 people and dine on a brief breakfast of whole fish, coffee, and hot bread with a hint of fresh berry jam.

6:30 A.M.

We enter the main assembly building, heated by 1950s-era diesel generators, for the day-long Gospel presentation. Audience seating is filled to capacity, the village's small hospital staff and interned patients the only no-shows. The village had literally shut down for the day, and nearly the entire population jammed into the auditorium and awaited the start of the program. Across the stage stood a long table with seats facing the audience in a panel formation. I was in the center with my 19-year-old translator on my right. He and I had the only two microphones. To my left sat the mayor, assistant mayor, and several regional VIPs. To my translator's right were the chief of police, his second in command, and several village VIPs.

7:00 A.M. TO 10:00 A.M.

I give a systematic presentation of Old Testament history showing God's blood-red thread woven throughout, heralding the coming Christ.

10:00 A.M. TO NOON

We conduct a well-participated Q & A session to make sure the audience has grasped God's redemption plan, including the complete Gospel summary that is Genesis chapter 5. The first question is from a very young boy in the first row: "When we are finished tonight, will you go and pray for my dying grandmother in the hospital?" We glance to the mayor and police chief; they both nod that I would be permitted to favor the little boy.

NOON TO 1:00 P.M.

We enjoy a sumptuous and plentiful picnic lunch.

1:00 P.M. TO 6:00 P.M.

I cover key points of the life, teachings, death, and resurrection of Christ, and the promise of His second coming, directly connecting all the points back to what I had just taught in the Old Testament.

6:00 P.M. TO 7:00 P.M.

We eat dinner and I continue to meet villagers and converse with local officials.

7:00 P.M.

We open the floor for any and all questions about God, Jesus, the Bible, the second coming, eternal life, and damnation. The attendees express their insatiable thirst for the truth by enthusiastically barraging us with questions about these spiritual matters.

8:30 P.M.

I give a thorough explanation of how I will lead the village in prayers of repentance and surrender, invite those who want to be reconciled to their Creator to stay, and dismiss those who do not. This night, only a family of nine persons leaves the auditorium. We later hear that they were the family of the local shaman priest and feared his reprisals.

Then I declare: "I know our Creator's favorite language on earth is Sakhali, but since I cannot speak that special language yet, I will pray aloud in English and my translator will pray my words in Sakhali. From your heart to God, repeat in Sakhali after him."

During the first outreach, at the moment of invitation, my translator freezes and I see color drain from his face. We cover our microphones with our hands, and in a voice trembling with terror, he says:

"Michael, I don't believe in my heart! How can I lead these people? Your God will strike me dead!"

I give him a gentle side hug, wink, and whisper, "Kolya, please trust me. God only needs your mouth right now, not your heart."

He brightens in a breath, and I know the Holy Spirit has comforted him. Kolya exclaims over the microphone, "I can do this!"

When we complete the prayers, a spiritual electricity fills the room, and the eager newborn saints pepper me with questions like, ""What do we do now for our Savior?" By the time we finish the impromptu discipleship session at 11:30 p.m., I am totally spent.

But we have yet to fulfill the request of the little boy in the front row ...

CHAPTER 33

Cleaning House at the Hospital

1999, a remote village in the Sakha Republic ...

A S SOON AS WE WRAPPED up the nearly 18-hour session, the little boy ran on stage, grabbed my hand, and led me, with my translator in tow, to the village hospital.

Upon entering the ramshackle building, I was assaulted with a thick bouquet of fresh lead-based paint, alcohol, and death. The boy led us down a long hall to a 20' by 20' room housing three elderly patients toeing the threshold of eternity. "Grandma" was barely exchanging what were surely her final shallow breaths.

I was pulling my small bottle of anointing oil from my pocket when we heard a loud and authoritative "STOP!" from the doorway behind us. The hospital administrator, flanked by two tough-looking nurses, curtly prohibited us from continuing and left the room.

With dread, we waited for his return, presumably accompanied by the mayor or police chief. But moments later we got a surprise. The hospital staff returned, bringing other patients to the room. They had indeed ordered us to stop—until they could gather all the patients to receive our prayers. For the next 15 minutes, they jammed all 50-plus patients into the room. They came in on beds, in wheelchairs, on crutches, and the few ambulatory patients walked or hobbled in and leaned against the walls.

I looked heavenward with nothing to offer God but my spent body. "Father, strengthen this vessel. I have no faith for this, but I obey You now."

I had my translator set a single chair in the center of the room, and through him I announced: "Only my God knows about, and can heal, every malady this night. I have no power except to be His instrument."

One by one, I anointed and prayed for every person in the room, beginning with the little boy's grandma. By 2:30 a.m. all had been prayed for and were returned to their rooms.

We hadn't returned to, or heard any news from, the village when, six months later, we were visited by a young, newly ordained Sakha pastor who had attended that one-day outreach.

Two days after we had left that village, he went to the hospital to check on the little boy's grandma. The hospital administrator met him at the door and, with wonder still resonating in his voice, said, "That grandma and all the other patients went home well the next morning. Our hospital is empty!"

CHAPTER 34

Teens Will Be Teens

1999, a village in the Sakha Republic ...

W HEN WE VISITED A VILLAGE during our evangelistic outreach, we typically convened a one- to three-
day event in a central meetinghouse previously used
regularly by the government during the Soviet era. The events were
scheduled a month or two in advance, so there was ample advance
promotion of our coming—and not a small amount of speculation
and rumor about what we were going to say.

We were invited by a village one winter for such a one-day event.
We arrived about 10 a.m. and stopped in front of the assembly
hall. It was padlocked. Without notice to us, the community decision makers had cancelled our event (our first ever cancellation)
and left the village for the day.

Despite the -50° F temperature, a small delegation of teenage
girls milled about the building, awaiting our arrival. As soon as
they recognized us, three of them ran to pre-assigned locations to
inform other girls in nearby buildings.

Within minutes, ten young ladies had crammed into our little four-wheel drive Russian van. Shortly afterward, an excited

teenage boy pressed his face against our windshield, saw all those young ladies, and ran off to gather the boys. It wasn't long before 19 teens muscled into that cramped space. We gave them each a Bible written in Sakhali, and for the next three hours, we presented a careful and thorough Gospel message and allowed them to ask any questions they wanted.

Afterward, as they were exiting the vehicle, I asked the last teen, who spoke excellent English, about the locked building and the youngsters' eagerness to wait outside to meet us on a very frigid Saturday morning.

She smiled broadly, and with a gleam in her eye, responded: "Many of the men in our village use that building to watch American pornographic films at night. They were very angry that the mayor invited you here to talk about the Bible. So they cancelled your event and told everybody they were going away so they didn't have to talk to you."

Though I probably should have known the answer, I asked, "But why did you young people wait around for us?"

"We couldn't wait to hear what you Americans had to say that would so scare our parents!"

CHAPTER 35

God 1, Principality 0

Winter 2000, Vilyuysk ...

D IANE: THE VAST AND SEEMINGLY endless territory of the Sakha Republic is demarcated by a host of
boundaries. Some are geographical, others political and
municipal. But supervening all those in both time and expanse is
a vast array of invisible boundaries reflecting ancient tribal do-
mains, spiritual principalities, and religious customs.

The tribal peoples are generationally steeped in the practice
of appeasing the spirits ruling over various areas by offering to-
ken gifts before venturing over one of the implicitly understood
boundary lines.

To call these rituals "superstitions" is to greatly understate their
spiritual and supernatural importance. An athlete wearing the
same socks or refusing to shave while his team continues its win-
ning streak engages in a harmless superstition. But making peace
with territorial spirits is invariably viewed by many tribal peoples,
including the Sakha, as a life-or-death necessity to invoke protection against human, natural, and spiritual threats.

It was the coldest day of the year when a Sakha teacher and I
prepared to travel 150 miles north to a remote village to speak at a

school and deliver much-needed food and supplies. We had not yet built a heated garage onto the side of our house, so before our driver could start our van, he had to crawl underneath the vehicle and heat the oil pan with a kerosene blowtorch.

After a while, he fired up the engine, we climbed in, and off we went along the crude road. About an hour into our journey, we approached a regional border crossing. Off to one side, I could see a large tree densely cluttered with hundreds of trinkets and scraps of colorful cloth. Our driver instinctively pulled off the road next to the tree and awaited the customary gesture of obeisance to the spirits.

My Sakha friend hesitated in her seat. She knew the obligatory ritual, but also recognized that I believed in a God greater than her local spirits. She looked at me, then at the tree. She looked at me again, then shifted her glance back to the tree. She repeated this visual volley several times before exiting the van, dutifully tying a piece of cloth to the tree, and quickly returning to her seat.

Expecting some judgmental reaction from me (we had talked many times about these customs), she braced herself for a rebuke, reproof, or lecture. But I merely smiled at her and quietly prayed that the Lord would watch over our travels. For the remainder of the trip, I prayed silently that my friend would see, through my life of faith, that my God was bigger than the regional powers and was well capable of protecting us from harm—without the benefit of offered trinkets and bits of fabric.

We shared a wonderful long day in the village, encouraging teachers and students and dining on delicious food so hospitably provided to us.

Our experience at the border crossing was different on the return trip. As we approached the border, my friend asked me to pray. I gladly accommodated with a brief petition for protection, which she affirmed with a confident "Amen!" We passed the tree without even slowing down, and my friend's four-decade old practice of appeasing the local spirits ended that day.

CHAPTER 36

Loaner Tools

2000, Vilyuysk ...

O N O C C A S I O N , W E R E C E I V E D unsolicited donations from the United States, and were always diligent to invest it in the lives of the people for their greatest benefit.

One such donation of $1,000 arrived in our account at the only bank in Vilyuysk. When I found out about the funds, I asked my best friend, "What's the greatest need for the most men in the village?" He spoke with a number of his extended family and friends and determined they needed power tools that were beyond their financial means.

Two weeks later, we made a trek to Yakutsk, where a German tool company had opened a power tool store in the city center. I purchased $800 worth of tools and about $200 in bits, blades, and small replacement parts.

I invited the men to a party at our house and, with a bit of fanfare, presented them with the tools, explaining through my translator that any of the men were welcome to borrow the tools, use them, and return them cleaned and in good working order. The men eagerly lined up, took the tools of their choice ... and that was the last I saw of that merchandise.

Six months later, the same men gathered at our home for another party. During the festivities, I noticed a group of five or six men pointing at me and laughing. I asked a translator to interpret for me and was told, "They are joking about the silly American who actually thought they were going to bring his tools back to him."

In response, I pointed a finger back at those men and laughed out loud. I asked the translator to tell them, "Those tools didn't belong to me. They had been donated through the hard earned money of American Christians. Therefore, the tools belonged to the God I serve and He delighted to make them available to those who needed them. So, those who were not returning them would have to answer to the Owner of the tools, not to me."

Within a week, all of the loan tools were returned—cleaned and in good working order.

CHAPTER 37

Say What?

Summer 2001, Vilyuysk ...

W HEN GOD CONFOUNDED THE LANGUAGES at Babel, He not only halted construction of the tower, He also set up a good share of laughs for Himself and His children.

While our daughter Bonnie was a student at my alma mater, Philadelphia Biblical University, she came to Vilyuysk to help us celebrate the annual summer festival and teach a summer Bible camp. In preparing her for her ministry there, we had cautioned her against using any of the multitude of American idioms to which we are so accustomed.

At the big summer festival, Bonnie got into a conversation with one of our best lady translators and spoke in passing of the joys of the Frisbee for a group of festival goers and picnickers in the United States.

"What is friz-bee?" Svetlana inquired blankly.

Bonnie responded enthusiastically, "Why, it's a fun toy that's better than sliced bread!"

Svetlana blinked in confusion and said, "What do you do with bread?"

Bonnie thought quickly and, emphasizing the idiomatic rather than the physical meaning, replied, "Well, it's universally loved—like peanut butter!"

Further frustrated, Svetlana asked, "Peanuts and butter?"

In a similar vein, I was babysitting our friends' 5-year-old daughter for a few hours in Yakutsk in 1998. This precious little girl had never been left alone by momma and papa, and she awoke from a nap to find "Da-dya" ("Uncle") Michael in the house with her. After searching the house, she began to cry softly, pining for her momma.

In my desire to comfort her, I exclaimed with as much compassion in my voice as I could muster, "Mamma coming!"

At that she screamed in rage, "Neee (No) momma comin'!"

I projected a reassuring joviality to lighten her hurt and anger as I repeated, "Da, momma comin'!"

We volleyed the same words for a few minutes until she started to hyperventilate. It finally dawned on me, *"Duh, this poor kid doesn't understand English,"* so I dropped the conversation. Even so, the girl continued stomping, kicking, throwing things at me, and fuming, "Nee momma comin'! Nee momma comin'!"

About an hour later momma and papa arrived. She ran to them and in no uncertain terms (though I caught only a few words of what she was saying) spat out her accusations against me to her father, apparently with the desire that papa would exact swift vengeance on mean Da-dya Michael.

Suddenly, papa—my best translator—burst into uncontrolled laughter. He related the problem to his wife and she came unraveled with laughter as well, with their only child standing there, betrayed and confused.

Apparently, my Yankee pronunciation of "Momma coming!" translated perfectly in Russian to "Your mother is (as stupid as) a rock!"

CHAPTER 38

Safe and Warm

Vilyuysk, early December, 2001 ...

DIANE: MY HEAVENLY FATHER HAD put on my heart to not only be a spiritual helper, but also to be equally available as a hands-on assistant whenever I perceived needs among the men. I considered it an honor to serve them.

"Pavel," a beloved young man who was a special helper in many facets of our village work, was charged with taking four mutual friends on a two-week winter fishing trip to replenish our stock. His uncle lent them his former Soviet troop carrier, a 3-ton truck converted into a hunting and fishing camper. It was routine to use our home to prepare and load for such trips.

When they finished stuffing the truck with food and supplies, the five men acted anxious to leave, but reluctant to partake in the final act of "the Christian lady's" routine. They halfheartedly shuffled towards me as I summoned them to join hands with me and pray. As our little circle closed, I suddenly sensed an overwhelming premonition of dread. Before I could discern the specific danger, I yelled for Michael to come down from our upstairs room.

He sensed the urgency in my voice, bounded down the stairs, and landed behind me seconds later. Without premeditation, I turned and directed him to quickly grab a Navy sea bag under our bed and fill it thermal underwear, socks, and other warm clothes. Before I began praying Pavel whined for all of them, "But Miss Diane, the truck is already packed and there is no room for—" He stopped in mid-sentence when I shot him the non-negotiable glare of a mother whose 5-year-old balks at wearing gloves in the snow.

Michael returned quickly with about 30 pounds of surplus clothing we had accumulated, as I prayed aloud that God would make His faithful love and protection tangible to them.

Six days later, Pavel walked into our home, shaken but glad to be alive, and told us a dreadful story. On the second day of their trip, while they were crossing a deep lake, the truck broke through the ice and was submerged in less than 30 seconds. When the truck broke the ice, one of them tossed the sea bag (which was in the cab with them because there was no other space for it) and some bread onto the frozen lake surface before the truck went under. The first escapee was strong enough to pull himself from the water onto hard ice; he then helped the others to safety. All of them were soaked to the skin in layers that were rapidly becoming rigid—and deadly. They quickly stripped off the lethal garments, put on the dry clothes, and hiked for 10 hours to a small cabin they knew of six miles away. There they subsisted for two days on the bread they had salvaged. Finally, some other men in a truck "happened by" and brought them back to us. All of the other provisions they had packed stayed at the bottom of the lake until the following spring when the truck was retrieved.

The very week of that incident, more than a dozen people died in our region when their cars or trucks broke through thin ice. Most froze to death in their wet clothes.

I took Pavel aside, looked him square in the eyes, and challenged him, "Were you ready to meet your God in the lake?"

His timid and recoiling answer was "No." So I urged him to thank God by using this second chance to really make his life count for eternity.

CHAPTER 39

Baptizing a 380-Pound Man

Beginning in 1998 in Yakutsk, and culminating in 2007 in a distant region in the northwest Sakha republic ...

O NE MORNING DURING OUR SECOND year in Ya-kutsk, one of my trusted drivers whisked me from my classroom. He drove me straight to a clothing store, bought me an "appropriate suit," and told me to put it on in the car as we sped through the city to a large auditorium.

I was quickly escorted to a raised podium where one of my favor-ite and trusted translators, dressed in his high-ranking federal uni-form, awaited me. As I approached the lectern, I turned toward the audience and saw a sea of 700 impatient faces. It was only then that I learned that I was a keynote speaker for a government-sponsored symposium for the Republic's top business leaders.

Though the government wanted me to wax eloquent on busi-ness practices in America, the Holy Spirit had a better idea, and prompted me to challenge the businessmen to carefully consider

God's business ethics. I spoke for about 40 minutes on business ethics from Scripture, and ended by sharing an experiment I conducted two years earlier.

On our second day living in Yakutsk, I took our first teaching advance in rubles and found the six closest markets to our home. In each, I found a small inexpensive item with its price clearly marked. In a deliberately clumsy attempt to point and pronounce what I wanted, I telegraphed myself as a vulnerable foreigner who could easily be taken advantage of. To purchase the small item, I offered a large denomination bill.

In five of the six stores the clerk (often also the owner) unhesitatingly shortchanged me to the tune of $7 to $9 U.S. At only one store was I treated honestly. There, a compassionate young clerk gently chided me for offering her such a large bill. She asked me to hold out my hand and she helped me count the exact amount I needed.

I had found the store I would shop at from then until we moved to Vilyuysk, and not once did they cheat me. The five other markets lost *all* our future business.

As I finished that story, my audience sat stunned and confused. No one had ever taught them that there could be any benefit to honesty?

After an obligatory and prolonged photo op with many members and groups from the audience, I was returned to my classroom. I had little hope in my heart that anything I said there would have an impact.

But nine years later and over 900 miles to the northwest, I was baptizing over 100 believers in a new church planted in an isolated region. On the second morning, the last 12 believers waited to be baptized. Last in line was a Sakha man of sumo wrestling stature.

When he entered the waist-deep water, I was absolutely certain I could dunk him, but wasn't at all sure I could bring him back up from the water. It was one of those moments I wished we were Presbyterian and I could just sprinkle him!

As we walked together out of the river, he asked, "Do you recognize me?"

"No, sorry, I don't," I replied.

He motioned his chauffeur over to us and directed him to show me "the picture." The chauffeur handed me a faded Polaroid of my newly baptized brother, my uniformed translator from Yakutsk, and me at the 1998 business symposium.

With great joy he told me the story of how my presentation had led him to faith in Christ. "I've been looking for you all these years," he said. When he heard where I was baptizing new Christians, he traveled two days to find me.

He ended his own testimony of God's handiwork. "God has changed my life, and my business is thriving, based on biblical principles!"

CHAPTER 40

Bringing it Full Circle

Early winter 2007, Yakutsk Airport ...

A MONG THE FIRST OF THE passengers through security and ticketing, I entered the cavernous gate area and, true to habit, sat in a seat against the back wall where I had a clear view of everyone who came into the terminal. I opened a favorite book and quickly withdrew myself from the cacophonous surroundings.

Within thirty minutes of boarding time, the 250-seat room was nearly filled to capacity with well-dressed businessmen, government officials, and military personnel. In the distance, I heard the unique click of high heeled shoes. In unison with the other men, I turned my head toward the entrance to see a stunning platinum blonde model in her twenties, dressed to devastate. My mind played the words and tune of an old 60s hit by Sam the Sham and the Pharaohs: "Little Red Riding hood / You sure are lookin' good / You're everything a big bad wolf could want / ow-woooo!"

As if orchestrated, the men sprang into action. Wedding rings were pocketed, posture improved, crude chatter ceased, and empty seats were cleared of briefcases and dusted. Clearly, all the male contestants were vying to be the lucky man to fly next to a sex goddess for the eight-hour flight to Moscow.

With an internal chuckle—and with heart and wedding ring unmoved—I resumed reading. Moments later I was attacked by a whiff of exotic perfume and the brush of an elegant fur coat. As I turned, my cheek received a wet glossy red kiss. Before I could react, the beauty laid herself across my lap, placed her head on my chest, then looked into my eyes with a childish grin and whispered in excellent English, "It's *me*, Michael, your Olga!"

Memories flooded my mind. Eleven years earlier, Diane and I had taught in several after school programs. How could I forget Olga, my most unforgettable 14-year-old classroom affliction? If class were in any way disrupted, Olga was certain to be the instigator. But a funny thing happened on the way to adulthood ... that gangly juvenile delinquent had blossomed into a gorgeous and elegant woman.

As soon as our flight was ready, Olga latched herself onto my arm and hurriedly dragged me to the gate. We were among the first to board, and she spirited me to the back of the plane. When we were seated, she collapsed in my lap, face buried in my shoulder, and began to sob deeply. I remained silent, waiting until she was ready to explain.

After her cathartic tear-burst, she reached into her purse for a hanky—and a pack of photographs. She apologized for the purgatory she had put me through in school and I smiled my forgiveness.

Then she added, "Do you remember your talk about abortion?"

"Yes I do, Olga."

She smiled and suggested something I had always hoped, "You know, I was only pretending not to listen." With that, she opened the pack of photographs ...

Just after Diane and I left Yakutsk, and only days after her 16th birthday, Olga was raped and left pregnant and terrified. Everyone in her life demanded that she abort the "thing" in her body.

But words from the classroom haunted her for nine months, *"Girls, God would be very sad if you ever killed the precious baby He would lovingly place in your womb."*

She proudly showed me a couple dozen photos of her healthy handsome boy. He is her delight and the joy of her mom and grandmother as the three of them raise him.

When Olga told me how often she prayed that Pastor Michael's God would allow her to find me and express the depth of her appreciation for her precious child, it was my turn to cry. Through my tears I encouraged her that, though God used my voice just once, His Holy Spirit repeatedly reminded her to protect His gift.

Olga granted me a great gift in return that day. I needed to be encouraged again that we truly had made an eternal difference in Siberia. And I was honored to serve as Olga's surrogate daddy to watch over her on her first solo trip to Moscow.

CHAPTER 41

Prepared for Daily Life in Siberia

DIANE: IN 1996, MICHAEL AND I entered the global community of Baby Boomer empty nesters.

For 21 years, I had built a nest for the four gifts God had given Michael and me through my womb. When I had to release our last child, Bonnie, to Bible college, my heart hurt deeply. My comfort-seeking heart made me afraid to go to Siberia, but I sincerely told God that if He opened the door, I would go. I asked Him if I should follow Michael to the northern Siberian wilderness, and He clearly spoke to my spirit, "No, Diane, I want you to follow *Me* there." From that moment the fear evaporated and I truly looked forward to going.

When we arrived in Siberia, God would not let me close my heart to others in sorrow for the "loss" of my four children. He opened my heart, and throughout our years in Siberia, students aged 13 through 28 would fight over who would take my arm and walk with me wherever we would go.

Our two-story log cabin was ready and waiting for us when we arrived in Vilyuysk. The Lord provided our home through a retired couple near Washington D.C. Their sacrificial gift purchased the cabin, the materials Michael needed to build all of our furniture, and a few basic appliances to ship up river from the big city.

The week we moved into our home, a Sakha family with three teenagers came to live with us. They all told me, "Just observe and join in when you felt comfortable." They were so very gracious to me. They showed me how to live without running water and limited electricity, and acclimated me to the many aspects of their daily life and routines. Though I was thankful for learning a level of simplicity from living in our school bus homes, life in the village was challenging on an entirely different level. Even in our bus homes, life was comparably easy and what I needed for housekeeping was always available with running water and electricity on demand.

I was truly blessed to release my rights and comforts in order to love and serve my Sakha family and students. The more I released myself to loving and serving them, the less impact the loss of comforts held in my daily life. We refused to have more or fewer things or a different lifestyle than our Sakha family had. We all lived the same life together.

Every week men and women from across the republic would come and spend time—sometimes days—with us, wanting to talk about the faith that would cause us to leave America and our family to bring a message to their people. One of their most frequent questions was, "Do the Sakha family and the American couple fight while living together, and if so what do you fight about?"

We would say, "Oh, yes, we have an ongoing disagreement in the home." That got their attention!

So we explained that the Sakha family insisted to all who inquired that the American couple was a gift from a loving heavenly Father. The American couple would immediately disagree, insisting that the Sakha family was their Father's special gift to them! This "argument" often opened the door to a clear Gospel message.

God had blessed Michael and me with a unique sovereign situation that would be most effective in conveying our love for Him in that place: Luke 10:3–9[27]. He gave us a whole family whose hearts were being softened by Him for eternal life and He gave us the honor of working together with Him and them in His Kingdom building.

Michael and I determined that even while the Sakha family took care of the practical issues of life in their world, we were to be their servants. Our rights, privileges, comforts, seniority (in years), etc., were never to get in the way of our humble service to their needs first.

Early one morning in our first month in the home, I dwelt upon a deep hurt and offense that in the scheme of our work there had little importance. The LORD spoke a clear rebuke to me that I immediately shared with Michael: *"You will never complain about your life here to my precious Sakha children. If you have a problem with anything, you and Michael come into the privacy of your bedroom and talk with Me about it."* That was how we were able to serve and bless our region in the love of Christ.

Everyday life was very different from what I had known during my 47-plus years in the States. I anguished to my Father, "Lord, can I really change and be like and identify with these precious people so I can tell them about you? Am I too old and set in my ways to change?"

Typically, our flesh reacts in one of two ways to what we don't know or understand, or to that which is different from what we are used to:

---

27. *Go your way; behold, I send you out as lambs among wolves. Carry neither money bag, knapsack, nor sandals; and greet no one along the road. But whatever house you enter, first say, 'Peace to this house.' And if a son of peace is there, your peace will rest on it; if not, it will return to you. And remain in the same house, eating and drinking such things as they give, for the laborer is worthy of his wages. Do not go from house to house. Whatever city you enter, and they receive you, eat such things as are set before you. And heal the sick there, and say to them, 'The Kingdom of God has come near to you.'*

1. We mock it, unwilling to acknowledge there may be validity or advantage to it.

2. We reject it outright, choosing to be repulsed by it because it thrusts us outside our comfort zone.

Those were my natural responses to many of the initial shocks in learning to live in a strange, harsh, and deadly place as my American comfort-centered life faded from relevance. But I clung to the promise of Philippians 4:12–13[28], turned my eyes to Jesus for guidance and strength, and focused my heart on loving my Sakha family. As I loved them, I also fell in love with how they lived and found the wisdom and joys of their ways. I am so grateful for all I learned from them.

No room of our cabin was ever messy, and although leftover food was kept in a pan on the floor, it was usually covered. The two teenage girls kept the home spotless; they always mopped the wooden floors with vinegar and water, and everyone took their shoes off by door, and donned house shoes for inside use.

The first and most important sustenance in village life is, of course, water. Global research and government agencies have confirmed with regularity that Vilyuysk lakes and rivers remain contaminated and unsafe for human consumption from Soviet nuclear bomb detonations in the region. Yet, with primitive chainsaws we cut ice from the river and put it in metal 55 gallon drums near the small indoor gas furnace that heated our house. Without any means of purification, we scooped the water into enamel bowls to make food or clean dishes. We used just a few drops of detergent in boiled water to wash dishes.

Our main staples—fresh horse, moose, and dozens of species of fish—were complemented at all meals with gravy over buckwheat, rice, or noodles. Lunch was usually moose soup with potatoes, noodles, onions, or sometimes borscht—cabbage, carrots, onions,

---

28. *I know how to be abased, and I know how to abound. Everywhere and in all things I have learned both to be full and to be hungry, both to abound and to suffer need. I can do all things through Christ who strengthens me.*

beets (and tomatoes when available). Bread was served at every meal. Even if rolls were available, they were supplemented by fresh bread (similar to our sourdough bread).

Among the Sakhas' favorite dishes is chicken—a rarity—with always available potatoes. They would chop the legs and other pieces into smaller pieces (they didn't eat chicken like we do). They also served fish soup, made from the whole heads of bigger fish. They took lake fish (almost like pan fish), removed the gall bladder (which made the fish taste bitter), stuffed the insides with rice, and cooked them in a skillet or pan on the stove. The intestine soup didn't taste so good at first, but it was so energizing that we learned to like it.

The Sakhas' absolute favorite treat was frozen cubes of raw horse meat. The horses, raised for food, were free from parasites, so the meat was clean. The people also make natural ice cream formed in small rounds, sometimes made only of cream, other times mixed with jam. A favorite for everyone was kefir, a sour milk specific to the region. Sour cream with homemade jam from a summer harvest was delicious on bread or homemade rolls.

We showed a long-term genuine appreciation for all their foods, and eventually they began to ask us about American foods, and we gradually introduced them to some of our favorites. We brought Rumford baking powder and peanut butter from the U.S. and American pancakes became a big hit and a regular Sunday treat, especially with maple syrup from the States. Our Sakha family inquired about what to put peanut butter on and Michael quipped, "Everything!" That was the wrong answer; they started putting peanut butter on everything (but they loved it). One of our favorite foods was my U.S. recipe for blueberry muffins made with the blueberries fresh from their forest.

Our last year in Vilyuysk, I introduced them to my American lasagna, which they absolutely loved; no matter how much I made, there were never leftovers.

For me, success in Siberia is empty apart from what God accomplished in me and through me to glorify Him. Following my Lord did not include seeking fame or notoriety—I merely walked in obedience—and continue to so to honor and glorify Him. That requires me to set aside possessions and comforts when He asks me to pursue higher goals. I serve an unseen, unfelt God whose past and present works in me reflect His will. Matthew 23:11[29] and Proverbs 11:25[30].

When I released having to be with our adult natural children, my Father gifted me with hundreds of new "children" whom I learned to love and who loved me as their American mom. My burning love for our Sakha family is only explainable through the verse that says the love of God constrains us. It was a love that God put in my heart for the people, and it has never left.

---

29. *But he who is greatest among you shall be your servant.*

30. *The generous soul will be made rich,*
And he who waters will also be watered himself.

CHAPTER 42

Taking Friendly Fire

L ITTLE DID WE KNOW THAT, in counting the costs of wholeheartedly serving our Lord and Savior, part of the price we would have to tot up would be the slurs and contempt of our spiritual siblings. But, in full disclosure of the particulars of our journey, we need to recount just a few examples of the friendly fire we took from the body of Christ. We do this in a spirit of exhortation, not condemnation. Satan means for us to become bitter and forsake the church and God, but we have learned to forgive and move forward in our Lord's service. Here is a representative sampling of our "misfortunes":

- During our second year at the Bible college near Philadelphia, we fellowshipped with a rural church until we were called into a closed meeting before the elders. We were rebuked and disfellowshipped for neglect of our family. Though all our family's daily needs were being abundantly met by God's provision, they considered it "inappropriate" for Michael to attend Bible college full time on the G.I. Bill and work only part time.

- During our ministry on the streets of inner-city Philadelphia, our children were enrolled in a church-sponsored

Christian academy. One school day, Michael went to the school to deliver a message to one of our children. They were not in the cafeteria with the rest of the student body, however. He found them eating in the principal's office. Though this had gone on for some time, they were ashamed to tell us that the pastoral staff decided they needed to be "punished" because their father—who claimed to be a Christian—wore his hair long and worked with drug dealers and street gangs throughout the night. The children of that kind of man, they reasoned, should not associate with the general school population.

- I (Michael) had been a youth pastor for only four months. We temporarily vacated our bus and settled our family into the church's parsonage and our children were attending their sixth week at their new school. Late on a Friday night, I received a phone call. On the line I heard the familiar voice of our pastor's wife, terrified, sobbing, and pleading, "My husband is beating and cursing our son and me again! Don't call the police, but will you please help us?" Then the phone went dead. The next morning, I privately approached the husband in his office about the call. He responded with cursing—and the next Sunday morning that pastor announced from his pulpit that I was no longer in my position and no longer welcome in the church or the parsonage.

- Diane was the beloved choir director of another church for a year while I (Michael) was a M.Div. student at Reformed Theological Seminary. The pastor asked me to teach Sunday school for their teens. I accepted, and from the start I taught Scripture as God's infallible and completely trustworthy testimony of Him and His will. In the second month, I was called into the pastor's office. He and his head deacon challenged me about my "silly" theology. They wanted no part of their kids being taught that the Bible was a book of real miracles and a God who sends people to a real hell. The following Sunday at a "special service," the pastor called me to the front during his sermon and mocked me.

- Fourteen years after we left Port Angeles, Washington, we were able to reconnect with old friends during a layover on our way to Anchorage, Alaska and then to Magadan, Russia. We quickly tracked down and went to see a dozen or so of our former close friends from the three largest churches we had attended. Without exception, every person we visited was stunned that Diane and I were together at their door. Within a week of our leaving in 1982, word had gone out that Mike and Diane had had a nasty divorce.

- Throughout our time in Russia, though we never advertised or promoted ourselves or our work, we nevertheless received almost weekly unsolicited messages from U.S. based foreign mission agencies and large wealthy churches who had somehow heard of us, rebuking us for pretending to be real missionaries since we did not "do" missions the accepted "American" way.

- In 2010, we shared our work in Sunday school at a large church we had visited eight years earlier. After church, an assistant pastor asked me (Mike) to come to his office the following Tuesday morning. When I arrived, he grilled me about a number of disturbing transgressions he alleged Diane and I had committed. I pressed him concerning his fictional accounts, and he retorted that, eight years earlier, I had given one of the members a "funny look." That member felt it his duty to assail our reputation with tales sure to wag the head. Interestingly, the pastor was unwilling to bring the talebearer to the meeting to talk face to face.

- In 2011, we were invited to avail ourselves of a ministry that counsels burned out pastors in a safe environment. We were assured that the counseling sessions were held in strictest confidence, but in less than six months, we discovered through some very uncomfortable encounters that strangers, saved and unsaved, throughout four counties had twisted versions of who we were. Their skewed versions of Diane contained elements of information shared only in confidence. I (Mike) never confided any personal information with my counselor since each of our sessions began with his wanting me to laugh along with him at the stupid predicaments his other counselees had told him in confidence. Up to that time I had learned through many years in ministry that anyone who used my ears as trash receptacles to dump in their trash talk of others, considered me fodder for the ears of others.

- The deepest hurt I "suffered" during our years in Siberia came during a solo trip in another part of Russia with two Sakha friends. The local motel we stayed in allowed a local pimp and his girls to live there and do business. The pimp paid the front desk clerk nightly for the list of foreign guests. Just before midnight I opened the door to a pimp speaking exceptional English with a half-dozen young girls in tow. I refused his offer for a girl and told him that I was a Christian. Without hesitation, he responded with pride, "No problem, American, we have Christian girls, Orthodox girls, Muslim girls…

About an hour later I found the pimp in the restaurant and asked about his response to my refusal. He said with smug confidence, "We have many Protestant Christian Americans who come without their wives to bring us God's Word…and we are confident while they are here that our girls will be busy."

I returned to my room and bitterly wept, "Father, forgive us."

EPILOGUE

A S WE PREPARED TO LEAVE Siberia for the last time, I (Mike) was given a two-week long series of thorough medical tests at the Austrian Medical Center in Yakutsk. At a final meeting of the department heads and hospital administrator, they handed my interpreter an official set of documents to be presented to the government officials charged with our well-being. The head physician gave an oral summation of the reports and punctuated his final statement with a shrug that caused my translator to erupt with laughter. His shrugged words were: "In summary, we don't know why he's still alive!"

I responded to the assemblage, "I know why. Our God is not finished with us yet."

Today we are back in the U.S., content with food and raiment (1 Timothy 6:8) with no residence or vehicle of our own, and all our possessions fitting in two suitcases each. We are thus available to go whenever and wherever Father sends us next.

We are continuing to avail ourselves by Internet to our spiritual charges among the Sakha. We do not know where the next day will take us—back to Siberia, back to pastoral ministry in the U.S., to another country, or perhaps to an entirely new type of work. We are not awaiting a new adventure, but continuing the one we began together in June, 1975: watching our daily divine appointments unfold from our Father's loving heart. Across the last 39 plus years of serving our Savior together we can summarize our journey in Paul's testimony in 2 Corinthians 6: 3–10.

Our fire for evangelism and our commitment to Christ by serving His kids has not waned. Pray with us as our Father leads us to His next chapter in "A Message Worth Dying For." For now our Father has not required us to lay down our lives for Him in physical death. Rather, He has required us to die to self every day in the bringing of His message. In our daily walk of crucifying our flesh, we yield up our appetites for what this world offers and find far greater joy and fulfillment in the contentment of *doulos* service:

Isaiah 55

◀ Michael in 1969 two weeks before salvation encounter at Marist Prep.

▶ Michael in 1979 on a Search and Rescue mission in the Coast Guard.

◀ Diane in 1969 first semester at Rollins College, Winter Park, FL..

▶ Wedding day 1975, Michael and Diane and both sets of parents Cocoa Beach, FL.

◄ Just purchased log cabin home in 1998 in Vilyuysk.

►Meagher family 1980 in Port Angeles, WA.

▲ Diane eating a raw snack 2000 in our Vilyuysk home.

▲ A Sakha dance troop of our pedagogical college students in Vilyuysk.

▲ A typical river crossings with our Russian van 2001.

▼ Baptizing 80 year-old believer in 2004.

▲ Baptizing new believer in 2007.

◀ Sakha leader and his daughter.

Part III: Biblical Reflections

Devotionals From a Different Angle
by Raymond L. Balogh, Jr.

with introductions by Michael Meagher

Note by Michael and Diane Meagher

During our meetings with Raymond in preparation for this book, we discussed a variety of topics in getting to know one another. At several points, the subject matter reminded him of devotionals he had written, which he read to us. We were struck by the fact that, despite our wildly different upbringings and journeys, we shared a commonality of spiritual experiences reflected through the devotionals. We invited him to include some of those devotionals in this book, and I (Michael) wrote introductions for each of them to indicate the bond of meaning and perspective we all share.

This devotional reminds me of the hours I spent during the dark Siberian winters, wrapped in furs, lying in the snow far from manmade light pollution, allowing Father's breathtaking celestial lightshow to melt my worries and cares, and worshiping the One I dubbed "Hanger of the Stars" ...

Starry, Starry Nights

Can you bind the cluster of the Pleiades, or loose the belt of Orion? ... Or can you guide Arcturus with his sons?
—Job 38:31–32

JOB HAD JUST UNDERGONE A rapid-fire bombardment of personal tragedies, so it's understandable that he would launch some sincere questions toward the God who allowed it all to happen. Still, when Job and his friends got a little big for their britches, the Almighty Creator returned volley by peppering Job with two chapters of unanswerable questions. Among the topics: geology, meteorology, animal behavior, and astronomy.

The questions above are intended as much for us as for Job, as they preceded by 3,000 years our scientific ability to verify the phenomena spoken of. The questions are all rhetorical, and the answers are all the same: *"Of course you can't, Job* [or insert your name], *but I, the Lord, already have."*

"Can you bind the cluster of the Pleiades?" The Pleiades, also known as The Seven Sisters, is actually a grouping of about 250 stars. In a configuration unique throughout the universe, the cluster is embraced by a cloud of gravity, and all the stars are gliding in lockstep along their chosen path. More than 25,000 scientific measurements confirm that "the Pleiades stars are kind of like a swarm of birds, flying together to a distant goal."

"Can you loose the belt of Orion?" The familiar alignment of stars that comprise Orion's belt is, astronomically speaking, merely a momentary happenstance. Those three stars are all moving in different directions, at different speeds, in different parts of the

universe. The band girding Orion is loosening as you read this, and in 10,000 years (a mere eyeblink in cosmos time), it will be completely dissolved and unrecognizable.

"Can you guide Arcturus with his sons?" Arcturus, one of the largest stars in the universe (several thousand times our own sun's mass), zips through the universe at an invincible 257 miles per second. Astronomers theorize that "the combined attraction of all the stars we know cannot stop him or even turn him in his path."

Who could possibly guide such a runaway behemoth? Only He who also scatters the stars of Orion. And ties together the bundle of the Pleiades. And choreographs the nightly dance of the awesome celestial wonders He flicked onto the cosmic stage "in the beginning."

><

We, as children of the Light, are privileged to approach those in the dark, gently take them by the hand, and walk with them toward the Heavenly Father.

Grasping the Speed of Light

A TEAM OF SCIENTISTS AT A Cambridge, Massachusetts research facility have slowed light "20 million-fold from 186,282 miles a second to a pokey 38 miles an hour." [*The Harvard University Gazette,* Feb. 18, 1999].

"In this odd state of matter, light takes on a more human dimension; you can almost touch it," said Lene Hau, a Harvard University physicist.

Little did she know ...

That was the true Light which gives light to every man coming into the world. He was in the world ... He came to His own. —John 1:9, 10, 11

When she heard about Jesus, she came behind Him in the crowd and touched His garment ... . Immediately the fountain of her blood was dried up, and she felt in her body that she was healed of the suffering ... . And He said to her, "Daughter, your faith has made you well. Go in peace, and be healed of your affliction." —Mark 5:27, 29, 34

The Light of the World, entirely unapproachable, unreachable, ungraspable in His glorified state, *made Himself of no reputation, taking the form of a bondservant,*[31] slowed Himself down and entered our muddy existence as one of us, just so He could be touched.

An ex-KGB colonel heard of our work in Siberia and addressed several members of the parliament as follows: "Two inconsequential Americans, like two tiny drops of water in a large pond, made an insignificant ripple that should have quickly faded as it moved outward. What puny difference should they have made? But strangely, even in their absence, the ripples continue to grow as they move out into our polar regions."

Crickets, Air Mass, and You

Now to Him Who is able to do exceedingly abundantly above all that we ask or think, according to His power that works in us ... —Ephesians 3:20

BELIEVE IT OR NOT, LIKE it or not, changing the world begins with you.

"But," you say, "I'm only one person. What can I possibly do?"

Well, the next time you lie back to enjoy summertime's evening symphonies, consider the cricket, an insignificant little creature that can emit a chirp audible for up to one-half mile in any direction.

31. Philippians 2:7.

As you know, the phenomenon of sound requires the movement of air. And a cubic yard of air (a box measuring three feet on each side) weighs a little over two pounds. That means, within its one-half mile dome of influence, the cricket is responsible for moving more than three billion pounds of air! How does this tiny creature move an air mass a hundred billion times its own weight?

It doesn't. By doing what it was created to do, the cricket merely moves the air closest to it, and God's creation accomplishes the rest.

So it is with you.

True, you are just one person, but you are never alone. Yes, you can only do one person's work, but your power does not stop with your strength. You see, God Himself amplifies every fraction of your spiritual obedience to proportions of degree and purity we can't even begin to comprehend.

Just do what you were created to do—at this time, in this place—and you will move more of your world than you ever dreamed possible.

Throughout our time and travels in Siberia and Russia, we were threatened by a vicious multiplicity of threats; we were bullied, robbed, cheated, molested, and poisoned. Yet not one of those weapons, often fired point-blank at us, destroyed us or hindered the Gospel message. Our God is not impressed by anything men, governments, or principalities try to do to keep His message from those He wants to reach.

The Fearsome Toothless Enemy

Having disarmed principalities and powers, He made a
public spectacle of them, triumphing over them in it.
—Colossians 2:15

A RIVETING ACCOUNT OF PRE-INVASION warfare off the coast of Sicily, as reported by World War II correspondent Ernie Pyle:

Our ship was about three and half miles from shore—which in the world of big guns is practically hanging in the cannon muzzle ... .

We'd been stopped only a minute when big searchlights blinked on from the shore and began to search the waters. Apparently the watchers on the coast had heard some sounds at sea. The lights swept back and forth across the dark water and after a few exploratory sweeps one of them centered dead upon us and stopped. Then, as we held our breaths, the searchlights one by one brought their beams down upon our ship. They had found their mark.

All five of them, stretching out over a shore line of several miles, pinioned us in their white shafts as we sat there as naked as babies. I would have been glad to bawl like one if it would have helped, for this searchlight business meant the enemy had us on the block. Not only were we discovered, we were caught in a funnel from which there was no escaping.

We couldn't possibly move fast enough to run out of those beams. We were within simple and easy gunning distance. We were a sitting duck. We were stuck on the end of five merciless poles of light, and we were utterly helpless.

"When that fifth searchlight stopped on us all my children became orphans," one of the officers said later.

Another one said, "The straw that broke my back was when the anchor went down. The chain made so much noise you could have heard it in Rome."

A third one said, "The fellow standing next to me was breathing so hard I couldn't hear the anchor go down. Then I realized there wasn't anybody standing next to me."

...

I don't know how long the five lights were on us. It seemed like hours, it may have been five minutes. At any rate, at the end of some unbelievably long time one of them suddenly blinked out. Then one by one, erratically, the others went out too. The last one held us a long time as though playing with us. Then it too went out and we were once again in the blessed darkness. Not a shot had been fired.[32]

Fellow Christian warriors, when the enemy levels his arsenal at you ... when you're sitting dead helpless in the crosshairs ... when he readies to pull the trigger ... Take solace in this glorious fact of warfare:

No weapon formed against you shall prosper ... [33]

In most cultures throughout the world, giving an inordinately expensive gift—particularly one that cannot be reciprocated—to a stranger or a glancing acquaintance is at best a puzzlement and at worst a grievous insult. So, the Sakha were at a loss how to respond to the Gospel we shared with them, a gift they deemed to be of incalculable value. They did their humble best by showering us with family heirlooms and other priceless treasures. Those gifts will remain on our "Wall of Honor" in Vilyuysk as trophies of God's inestimable love for us and for them.

A Precious Vile Mess

You were not redeemed with corruptible things, like silver or gold ... but with the precious blood of Christ, as of a lamb without blemish and without spot. —1 Peter 1:18, 19

I N EARLY JANUARY 2006, ON a remote southern Australian beach, a recently unemployed fisherman and his wife found a 32-pound glob of strange substance.

---

32. From Brave Men, pp. 21–22.

33. Isaiah 54:17.

What they found was ambergris, a gastrointestinal secretion produced by sperm whales to disgorge digestive irritants. According to anecdotal evidence, its upheaval is accompanied by an unearthly commotion audible for miles. Fresh ambergris bears a horrendous odor, resembling a mixture of manure and alcohol. Ambergris is, in essence, vile, stinking, disgusting whale vomit.

But, with a jaw-dropping irony only God could have concocted, it is also worth a fortune. Mr. and Mrs. Fisherman's find would have traded about $10 an ounce higher than gold the day it was discovered.

Who would shell out such an exorbitant price for such a nauseatingly unattractive product? Believe it or not, the perfume industry, because cured, processed ambergris loses its odor and provides a fixative quality to any perfume to which it is added. And only those who already know its value and purpose are going to place their bids.

Imagine the most vile, stinking, disgusting person you know (even if that is yourself). Who on earth would pay a price higher than gold for such an individual?

He already did. And He didn't leave us guessing about His market price.

❧

All of us suffer from "I" disease, an intractable cancer that must be daily checked by the chemotherapy of God's Spirit in and through His Word.

"That Just Isn't You"

But if I am doing the very thing I do not want, I am no longer the one doing it, but sin which dwells in me. I find then the principle that evil is present in me, the one who wants to do good. —Romans 7:19-20

Vince Neil, lead vocalist of the heavy metal band Mötley Crüe, chronicles the heart-shattering details of helplessly watching his 4-year-old daughter, Skylar, fight a losing battle with cancer. Enduring radiation treatments, several doses of chemotherapy, and six operations, little Skylar languished for five months in increasing pain before succumbing to the disease. Neil describes the gruesomely inevitable:

After the [final] operation, she went into a fast decline: her lungs, her left kidney, and her liver all began a mutiny, refusing to function properly. Mercifully, she soon slipped into a coma. Her little body just couldn't take any more. It had been cut open and sewn back up so many times; it had been pumped so full of drugs; it had been shot through with more radiation than anyone should be exposed to; it had endured the slicing, dicing, rearranging, scraping, and removal of so many of its contents that, like a brake that has been pressed over and over, the parts had worn away and no longer knew how to work together.[34]

At one point, Neil meets the enemy:

They had successfully removed the tumor: it weighed six and a half pounds. That's how much Skylar had weighed when she was born. I couldn't even conceive of something that immense growing inside her. I wanted to see what was killing my daughter, so I asked the doctors if they had kept the tumor. They brought me down to the pathology lab, showed it to me, and my stomach turned. I had never seen anything like it before: It was the face of evil. It lay spread out in a metal plate . ... It looked like a gelatinous football that had been rolled through the depths of hell, collecting vomit, bile, and every other dropping of the damned that lay in its path. It was, in every conceivable way, the exact opposite of the daughter Sharise and I had raised.[35]

---

34. From The Dirt, p. 300.

35. From The Dirt, p. 299.

No one can doubt that Vince Neil loved his daughter whole-heartedly and hated that cancer with equal ferocity. He knew that the two were not one and the same; in fact, they were nothing at all like each other.

The only way we can accept that "God loves the sinner but hates the sin" is to realize that He sees us as separate from our sin. The Deceptive One has reliably convinced many of us (even under the guise of "righteous humility") that we are "sinners" in the sense that sin is melded to our beings even more than the cancer was intertwined with Skylar's vital organs. We begin to doubt God's unconditional love for us when we stop recognizing sin as a virulent but foreign intruder and accept it as an unwelcome but inexorable part of our essence.

But cancer never was a part of who Skylar really was, and sin is not an ingredient in our self-definition. That's not how—or why—we were created.

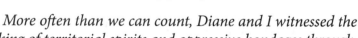

More often than we can count, Diane and I witnessed the breaking of territorial spirits and oppressive bondages through the speaking of one short passage of Scripture. The next two devotionals give vivid pictorials of that reality.

A 600-Year-Old Obstacle

And the apostles said to the Lord, "Increase our faith." So the Lord said, "If you have faith as a mustard seed, you can say to this mulberry tree, 'Be pulled up by the roots and be planted in the sea,' and it would obey you." —Luke 17:5–6

WELL, THEY HAD TO ASK ...
You've heard about how small and pungent the mustard seed is, but have you considered the thing in the crosshairs of that kernel of faith?

Mulberry trees are staunch, sturdy hardwoods. They grow to a height of 30 feet; have an extensive, stubborn root system; and often live up to 600 years.

Jesus wasn't impressed. He probably even had a particular tree in mind (... "this mulberry tree" ...), most likely pointing it out when He spoke those words.

You want to get rid of an obstacle in your life? Then do what He said.

It doesn't matter if the thing is bigger and harder than you.

It doesn't matter how deep its roots go.

It doesn't matter how long it has been there.

Command it in faith, and be sure to toss it where you're unlikely to see it again.

Knocking Slavery Down a Peg

You will know the truth, and the truth will make you free ... Everyone who commits sin is the slave of sin ... So if the Son makes you free, you will be free indeed. —John 8:32, 34, 36

ATTACHED TO THE WALL OF the chapel at Oakwood Park Conference Center in Syracuse, Indiana, commemorating one of the camp's founders, is an ox yoke.

You know how they work. A thick wooden beam is placed across the shoulders of the animal, and a U-shaped wooden bow is looped under its neck, passed through holes in the cross beam, and secured with wooden pegs.

But do you know how they really work? The truth is that the ox is not enslaved by the yoke. The ox is enslaved by the pegs that fasten the yoke. Thousands of pounds of powerful, obstinate beast held in check by a couple of pencil-sized sticks a child could snap in two.

You don't have to outmuscle, outsmart, or outmaneuver the yoke. Zero in on the pegs. Remove them and the yoke drops harmlessly to the ground.

It doesn't take a lot of truth to set you free. Only enough to remove the pegs.

Sigh. Indeed, some experiences are universal. I suppose every parent at one time or another has had to embrace a precious child's unavoidable pain as their own.

My Favorite Teacher: Lesson 1

Though He slay me, yet will I trust Him. —Job 13:15

MY DARLING DAUGHTER WAS JUST a toddler the Christmas I had to hurt her to protect her from harm.

We were in the living room. I was wrapping presents and she was just barely within arm's reach near the Christmas tree. She picked up something shiny, and was about to put it in her mouth. I looked up just in time to see that the curious bauble was a jagged shard of a broken glass Christmas ornament. I had just enough time to shout, "No!" and slap the danger out of her grasp.

For the brief moment before she burst into tears, she drilled me with a heart-rending look of shock and anger, betrayal and confusion. If she could have expressed her cauldron of emotions, she would have said, "Daddy, why did you hit me? I don't understand. I thought you loved me. All I wanted was to taste and enjoy that shiny thing." As if that moment weren't already indelible, the sunlight through the window punctuated her glare. I have never since seen her eyes blaze so blue.

Then she hung her head and began bawling.

But what she did next truly melted my heart. Amid her soul-wrenching sobs, there arose deep within her heart an uncomprehending trust in the one she could neither understand nor fight … and she reached up for me to hold her.

She needed love.

She needed comfort.

She needed me.

I scooped her into my arms and we cried together. Soon the trauma was over, and our relationship, broken from only one direction, was restored.

Far more often than you realize, when your heavenly Father slaps your hand, He doesn't do it out of anger. But sometimes you leave Him no choice but to hurt you so you don't harm yourself. It is at that moment when you need to reach up to the Author of your pain and let Him set things right for you.

～～

One summer night, Diane and I found ourselves in an unfamiliar region by an uncaring "taxi" that stranded us (permanently, for all we knew) in a mosquito infested swamp far from any village. We had no food, clean water, shelter, or means of communication. After 10 hours, two haggard men—who had been released a few days before from a gulag 20 miles away—emerged from the forest edge and approached us. They quickly introduced themselves and within 15 minutes had built a fire, distilled two liters of murky river water, and shared with us their last box of Chinese instant noodles. These two prison-hardened guardian angels stayed with us for the remainder of our ordeal, protecting, serving, and comforting us. He always provides.

Providing Manna Without Skipping a Beat

And the children of Israel ate manna forty years, until they came to an inhabited land. —Exodus 16:35

GOD SUPERNATURALLY PROVIDED FOOD IN a barren desert for an entire nation for an entire generation— and didn't miss a meal.

How many meals? Well, the nation of Israel during their wanderings consisted of about 600,000 men of fighting age, not including women, children, or the handicapped or infirm. A good, fair estimate places 3 million people crossing the Red Sea and heading into the wilderness.

And, as certain as the rising sun, God provided manna from above, 40 years straight, for their morning and evening meals. So, 3 million meals twice a day[36] for 40 years ...

That's 87,600,000,000 (that's billion, with a "b") servings faithfully endowed upon an unfaithful, often ungrateful people.

One of His names means "The God Who Provides." Boy, He wasn't kidding.

Many times we didn't know where our next meal was coming from. But it was always there, ready and waiting, as soon as we took the time to sit at His table.

"Give Us This Day"

So He said to them, "When you pray, say: '... Give us this day our daily bread.'" —Luke 11:2, 3

---

36. Technically, God provided no manna on the Sabbath day of each week, but He always sent a double portion the day before.

A FRIEND OF MINE (our daughters attended school together), returned from chaperoning a local high school's annual two-week field trip to Civil War battle sites.

I knew that he, a knowledgeable Civil War buff, would enjoy the learning experience, probably more than the kids would. So, expecting to learn second-hand about that fascinating epoch of American history, I was eager to ask, "So, how did the trip go?"

"It was great," he answered, and then immediately zeroed in on the aspect of the trip nearest his heart. Casting a genuine, satisfied smile, he said, "I got to see my daughter every day."

"Don't tell me," I said, "I know how you arranged that. You doled out her spending money one day at a time."

"That's exactly what I did. But how did you know?"

My friend needn't have been surprised. He knows that giving isn't enough; it is only one ingredient of the relationship we crave with the children we love.

You fathers understand.

So does He.

That's why He wants us to pray for our daily bread. He so savors a continual relationship with us, He doesn't want to wait past tomorrow for us to talk with Him.

>⌒⌒⌒⌒

For me it was a bicycle; for Raymond it was a car. But it is one and the same God who watches over us as ...

The Split-Second God of the Universe

But the Lord is faithful, who will establish you and guard you from the evil one. —2 Thessalonians 3:3

I WASN'T IN A HURRY, and I was dutifully obeying the posted speed limit. I just had other things on my mind.

So I didn't realize I had run the red light until the Honda Civic plowed into the front left fender of my car and knocked me to my senses. I wasn't hurt, and the other driver was just slightly dazed, with negligible injuries.

It surprised me that my first thought wasn't "Why did this happen to me?" but rather "Why wasn't this much worse than it was?" In fact, why aren't our lives much worse than they are? With a hateful enemy rabidly trying to destroy us, why isn't he more effective in his relentless assaults?

In that mercifully uneventful collision, my Heavenly Father taught me two powerful lessons:

1) We live under a thick blanket of God's benevolent sovereignty. Just as a fish doesn't know what it means to be wet, we are often so protected that we don't even know how secure we are. Sometimes, when we take that safety for granted (and maybe get careless and stupid), He has to lift a corner of that blanket to show us the dangers that constantly swirl about us.

2) His lovingkindness is as intimate as it is universal, and we are the undeserving recipients of His personal concern and care.

A car traveling 30 miles per hour covers 44 feet a second. Had I proceeded through that intersection one-tenth of a second earlier (or left my apartment one-tenth of a second earlier, or stepped out of the shower one-tenth of a second earlier), the Civic would have slammed me squarely in the driver's door, with gruesome results I don't care to contemplate.

It gloriously boggles the mind that a Creator who deals routinely in light years and millennia is faithful enough to take notice of one-tenth of a second and a few feet to protect one of His billions of children.

Every people group on Earth has found a way to debase all other groups over real or imagined differences—differences that are dwarfed by our sameness in the eyes of the Father.

As a God-ordained antidote to such hate and prejudice, Diane and I sang—in Russian, Sakhali, Hebrew, and English—of the divine harmony spoken of in Psalm 133.[37]

Now Open Wide and Say "Ah"

And because you are sons, God has sent forth the Spirit of His Son into your hearts, crying out, "Abba, Father!"
—Galatians 4:6

A CCORDING TO The *Guinness Book of Records* under Language, Commonest Sound: "No language is known to be without the vowel 'a' (as in the English 'father')."[38]

Or, as in the Aramaic "Abba."

"Abba" is the equivalent of Daddy or Papa. According to Vine's Expository Dictionary, "Abba is the word framed by the lips of infants and betokens unreasoning trust."

Slaves and servants were not allowed to address their master by that name. Only family members could do that.

And don't be surprised if "Daddy" is His favorite title. Perhaps that's why He has literally equipped every people and tribe and tongue and nation to begin to call out to Him: "Ah— ... "

---

37. *Behold, how good and how pleasant it is*
For brethren to dwell together in unity!

It is like the precious oil upon the head,
Running down on the beard,
The beard of Aaron,
Running down on the edge of his garments.

It is like the dew of Hermon,
Descending upon the mountains of Zion;
For there the Lord commanded the blessing—
Life forevermore.

38. 1992 edition, p. 171.

But you have to be part of the family to finish the word, and His children can do that only by His grace.

After all, we went from enemies (Romans 5:10) ...

... to slaves (Luke 17:10) ...

... to friends (John 15:15) ...

... to adopted children (Romans 8:14–16) ...

... to joint heirs (Romans 8:17) ...

... to co-rulers with Christ (2 Timothy 2:12).

Now that's something to thank Papa for.

Karasee, French toast, or God: we can't properly enjoy them without our Great Physician preparing our palates.

News Flash:
Hospital Food Gets Bad Rap

O taste and see that the Lord is good. —Psalm 34:8

I LOVE FRENCH TOAST. I prefer it slathered with butter and drizzled with real maple syrup. But even a bald, unadorned piece, browned to perfection, is a treat to me.

One summer half my lifetime ago, I spent three days in the hospital following a lawn mower accident. (I am happy to report that, although not unscathed, all ten toes are still alive and, ahem, "kicking.")

Having had no food the first two days, my appetite returned the morning of Day Three, when I felt at least marginally well enough to eat. When presented the list of breakfast options, I was delighted to find—you guessed it—French toast.

I feebly but enthusiastically cut the first forkful and put it in my mouth to savor the taste. Ugh! It was awful! How could anything be so blandly tasteless and still taste so bad? I set down the fork and nudged the tray away, chalking up my disappointment to another recuperating victim betrayed by that perennially maligned cuisine known as "hospital food."

But, really, there wasn't anything wrong with the food. The fault was entirely mine. With bodily systems sloshed in medication and scrambling to recover from a major trauma, I was simply incapable of enjoying a simple gustatory pleasure. The problem wasn't the food. My taster just didn't work right. True, hospital food may not be seasoned as much as we'd like, but the main reason it gets such a bad rap is that people are sick, diseased, or otherwise physically traumatized when they eat it.

So it is with God. He hasn't changed. He offers the same sweet, delicious fulfillment to everyone who will venture to taste His goodness. All too many of us spit Him out and blame Him for leaving a bad taste in our mouths. The rejection may be brusquely intellectual, violently emotional, or listlessly apathetic, but the blame is always misplaced.

You want to enjoy feasting on God's goodness? You may have to ask the Great Physician to heal your taster first.

✎

Son Michael Jr. was fearless when testing the limits of large playground equipment. One day, when he was nine, I was at a home improvement store when the Holy Spirit strongly urged me to immediately go to a friend's home where my family was visiting. I parked my half-full cart to a corner of the store and rushed over there. I arrived to see a growing crowd of onlookers closing in on Michael Jr., who had gashed his leg on a swing set. He kept calling for me, and was told repeatedly that I was not there. Undaunted, he persisted: "I don't care! Dad!" No one could get him to move until I arrived. His fear left, confidence reigned, and it seemed his pain lessened when Dad took charge. How often I have looked for my heavenly Dad's face when He alone needed to take command of my plight.

My Favorite Teacher: Lesson 2

My heart said to You, "Your face, LORD, I will seek."
—Psalm 27:8

O NE WEEKEND I TOOK MY sweet little daughter to the ball park where I played fast-pitch softball. I took a seat in the bleachers behind home plate to watch a game, and told her she could play nearby.

As I watched her, I witnessed a common childish phenomenon. She would find something of interest and toddle over to take a look. Shortly, some other fascination would capture her attention, and she would abandon her current discovery to check it out. This was followed by another diversion, and another, and another ... all in the same general direction—away from me.

Before too long, this conspiracy of serial distractions led her to a place beyond where she had ever been before. She looked up and instantly realized her lostness. Panic creased her face as she turned and scanned the crowd of strangers. The small, earthy things that had captivated her moments earlier no longer held any sway whatsoever, and she wholly devoted herself to searching for the only thing that mattered—my face.

Our eyes locked, I smiled at her, and both her worry and the distance between us instantly evaporated. Though still in unfamiliar territory, she was no longer adrift; she was anchored by the assurance that I knew where she was.

And just like that, her world was set right again.

The next two devotionals express our purpose in ministering to the Sakha people, many of whom initially—and wrongly—thought we were there to impose upon them a new set of "God regulations"—dos and don'ts, rites and rituals, and pious conformity to the dead letter of the law. We were careful to examine ourselves first ...

"There's a Right Way and a Wrong Way ... "

Reference: Luke 18:9–14

ALSO HE SPOKE THIS PARABLE *to some who trusted in themselves that they were righteous* (there's nothing wrong with thinking we're righteous, as long as we recognize that our righteousness is in Christ[39]), *and despised others* (here they went too far by looking down on others):

"Two men went up to the temple to pray, one a Pharisee (one of the white-collar power brokers of the day, highly esteemed among his own and envied by those of lesser status) *and the other a tax collector* (one of the loathsome bottom-feeders of the day, as regarded by almost everyone). *The Pharisee stood and prayed thus with himself* (this isn't starting out well. Jesus didn't even consider that this guy's prayers went any further than his own prideful heart).

'God, (now count the "I"s) I thank You that I am not like other men—extortioners, unjust, adulterers, or even as this tax collector (he notices who else is praying, but he really should have just minded his own business). I fast twice a week; I give tithes of all that I possess.' (This isn't a prayer; it's an assault. Well, good for him, I suppose, but what did he ask for? What was the point of this prayer? No wonder his words never got past the ceiling of the temple).

And the tax collector, standing afar off, would not so much as raise his eyes to heaven, but beat his breast, saying, 'God (and here the

---

39. 2 Corinthians 5:21.

similarity to the previous prayer ends), *be merciful to me* (no "I"s as the subject in this prayer; just a single "me" as the object of God's hoped-for mercy) *a sinner!' I tell you, this man went down to his house justified rather than the other* (Not "more justified." Only one was justified; it wasn't merely a matter of degree); *for everyone who exalts himself will be humbled, and he who humbles himself will be exalted."* (This sounds all backward to the self-sufficient, but it's the only way it works).

Now for the real hoot: Jesus offered this despicable Pharisaical caricature to the very audience most likely to say, "Boy, thank God I'm not like him!" He was probably in the next town by the time they figured out He was talking about them.

Who are you glad you're not like? And are you absolutely sure you have a right to feel that way?

❧

... As Diane and I gave all that we had; He abundantly added much more ...

Getting Way More Than You Asked For

Reference: Acts 3:1–8

N**OW, PETER AND JOHN WENT** up together to the temple at the hour of prayer, the ninth hour. (3:00 p.m. by modern reckoning. The two disciples were on their way into the temple for a regularly scheduled religious observance. But, "a funny thing happened on the way to church ... ") *And a certain man lame from his mother's womb was carried,* (this poor fellow had literally never been able to carry his own weight, but that is about to change) *whom they laid daily at the gate of the temple which is called Beautiful,* (Much about the shame and degradation beclouding this man is unspoken here. He also had to rely on family members, friends, or anonymous Good Samaritans to transport him to the bathroom. They had to do his shopping and chores, and he was utterly dependent on them to bring him food and drink, and to help him change his clothes. He had little privacy, and his dignity was thoroughly shredded) *to ask alms from those who were entering the temple* (hoping to scrounge just enough pocket change to get through the day, from passers-by whose compassion was blunted by the frequency of requests from the man and others similarly suffering).

When he saw Peter and John about to go into the temple, he asked to receive alms. (He was about to be healed, but his paradigm was fixed from his birth: he would never walk, and could only expect a trifling hand-to-mouth pittance.) *What are you daring to ask God for? Have your expectations been funneled into the "that's the way it'll always be" trap?*

And fixing his eyes on him, with John, (They stopped to concentrate on the man and his needs. This was more important than getting to the church on time.) *What detours or delays would you accept on your way to church? Peter said, "Look at us."* (The lame man doesn't know it yet, but his miracle was starting from the inside out. Requesting eye-to-eye contact from someone steeped in shame and inferiority may just be the first step to greater healing and awakening.) *When ministering to a drug addict, vagrant, prostitute, or jail inmate, do you ever call the outcast "Sir" or "Ma'am"? Why not?*

So he gave them his attention, expecting to receive something from them. (Well, perhaps that's progress. He went from requesting alms to expecting ... well, "something." What did he see in the disciples' eyes that flickered his hope?) *What do the needy sense in you that raises them to the next level of expectation?*

Then Peter said, "Silver and gold I do not have, but what I do have I give you: In the name of Jesus Christ of Nazareth, rise up and walk." ("Forget the mundane trifles, sir, the Abundant Lord of the Universe wants you to have stratospherically more than you've ever imagined.") *How often do you go beyond the surface requests of the needy? All you have—and all you need—is faith in the power of the name of Jesus.*

And he took him by the right hand (symbolic of the right hand of fellowship) *and lifted him up* (you could hardly blame the lame man for needing the nudge), *and immediately his feet and ankle bones received strength. So he, leaping up, stood and walked and entered the temple with them—walking, leaping, and praising God.* (And so God answers the unspoken prayer, and the faith of his instruments, with characteristic generosity. Even Peter must have been surprised; he only said, "Rise up and walk." But God did so much more to enable the man to jump up and leap around. Besides muscular strength, He bestowed balance, coordination, flexibility, and the interconnectivity of stimuli and brain function. You really couldn't have expected that.)

Or could you ... ?

❧

From start to present, Diane and I have done our best to fulfill Matthew 25 by meeting those physical and spiritual needs represented by each lack Jesus described. We did so, however, not by our provision. Father assured us that if we would be His conduits with open hands and hearts to receive—He would equally enable us to give.

"I Wouldn't Ask You to Do What I Haven't Done Myself"

Then He will also say to those on the left hand, "Depart from Me ... for I was hungry and you gave Me no food; I was thirsty and you gave Me no drink; I was a stranger and you did not take Me in, naked and you did not clothe Me, sick and in prison and you did not visit Me."
—Matthew 25:31–46

W ELL, ISN'T THAT A BIT harsh? After all, what did He ever do for us?

"*I was hungry* ... " We weren't just hungry. We were starving to death, malnourished beyond repair, sinking fast. To make matters worse, we insisted on drip-feeding ourselves with the deadly cocktail of "*the lust of the flesh, the lust of the eyes, and the pride of life.*"[40] Then came the Bread of Life, the Manna from Above, and offered us no less a live-giving feast than He Himself. Now we can have life abundantly here and feast on His wedding banquet on the other side.

"*I was thirsty* ... " We weren't just thirsty. We were parched beyond measure, desperate for just one fingertip of cool water to ease our torment. Our mouths were so dry, we were incapable of even tasting His goodness. (Without moisture, the human palate is incapable of taste). Then He came and poured out for us a flowing fountain of living water. "Whoever drinks of the water that I shall give him will never thirst. But the water that I shall give him will become in him a fountain of water springing up into everlasting life."

"*I was a stranger* ... " We weren't just strangers, and we weren't just wandering astray by innocent blunder. We were aliens by our own choice. We turned our back on the King, declared ourselves competitors for the throne, and entrenched ourselves for the battle. Then came the Good Shepherd, Who had long sought us out before taking us in. And, He not only took us in, but He purchased our adoption as children of the Everlasting Father. Now we can call Him "Abba, Daddy," a name allowed to be uttered only by true sons and daughters of the Master.

"*I was naked* ... " We weren't just naked. We were fully exposed to the core in our sin and shame, vulnerable and without answer to the ruthless accusations of the enemy. We were without merit, without defense, and without any means to pay for our crimes. Then came the Lamb of God, the Great High Priest, who paid

---

40. 1 John 2:16

the once-for-all sacrifice, exposed to the world while His garment was being gambled away beneath the cross. He will clothe us in white robes of righteousness forevermore.

"I was sick ... " We weren't just sick. We were as good as dead, riddled to the core with the lethal cancer of sin. Without any strength of our own, we were utterly incapable of stopping our inevitable plunge into the abyss. Then came the Great Physician with His life-saving blood transfusion. Exchanging His life for ours, He sustains us moment by moment, holding our very breath in His hand.

"I was in prison ... " We were imprisoned by an enemy far too powerful for us, destined for final execution, not even knowing where to look for a way of escape. Then came our Savior, our Redeemer, our Liberator, who didn't just visit us, but released us from our shackles, shattered our chains and bonds, and placed us in the heavenlies with Him, far above the reach of our former captor.

Now, to the best of your capability, and with His sovereign and enabling Spirit: go and do likewise.

Part IV:
Appendix

Letter to Diane

31 MAY 1975
(28 DAYS BEFORE OUR WEDDING)

MY DEAREST DIANE,
Well, God bless you, sweetie! It's Saturday morning, and I'm just sitting here in the office having a little Bible study. I don't have to work this morning, so there is nothing to do but have sweet fellowship with my Lord Jesus. An officer walked in about fifteen minutes ago and couldn't believe there was someone willing to give up a Saturday morning of TV, sleep, or a good card game with the guys for Bible reading! It is a bit difficult to explain to them that reading scriptures over and over again can be exciting and fulfilling. Actually I do not have any problem explaining it; they just have a hard time believing it!!

I have been very blessed this morning in what the Lord has shown me. You are becoming so precious to me, Diane, that I don't feel that the Lord has gotten His message to <u>all</u> of me until I have shared it with you. It seems that my spirit is beginning to develop an enormous appetite for the Word of God. I pray that this God-given thirst and hunger continues to grow. To be able to lead you into a deeper and more meaningful walk with the Lord, I can't afford to let my prayer life stagnate.

I realize that what I am going to share with you may seem a bit old or repetitious to you; but to me, I continually get excited and expectant in this area of our life in the light of God's Word. I was reading from the Gospel of Matthew, the entire sixth chapter. Please read it if you have a Bible handy. Pay particular attention to verses 7&8; 19–21; and 25–34. Every word of that chapter—especially the above verses—really fill my spirit with joy. You know what makes it really neat? Jesus meant EVERY WORD OF IT!!

He also has the love, the power, and the desire to fulfill EVERY WORD OF IT. One of the best verses in the chapter is verse 8:

"BE NOT THEREFORE LIKE UNTO THEM, FOR YOUR FATHER KNOWETH WHAT THINGS YE HAVE NEED OF BEFORE YOU ASK HIM."

Wow, isn't that fantastic? Too many times our wants have a way of distorting our needs. We have a tendency of forgetting that enormous difference between needs and desires. If we don't watch it we are going to miss out on many God-given needs met, because we wanted something else that appealed to the eyes. The Lord's Prayer is PERFECT! Jesus showed us right there what our needs are. "They will be done in earth, as it is in heaven ... " seems to be all inclusive of everything we might ever need besides the bread, and the principles of forgiveness and temptation. What right do we have to tell God what He will or won't, can or can't give us? I don't as yet understand the full implications of verse 24 of chapter 6, but I have a very strong leading to believe that the Lord was laying a real heavy saying on us. One master will soon fade away, and the other will be in the business of blessing and supplying for eternity. Really look long and hard at verses 25–34! IS JESUS REALLY SERIOUS? IS HE TRYING TO PUT US ON, DIANE? What are you and I going to do about these commands that He has given us? I am being very frank. These words of our precious Lord and Savior may just revolutionize our lives. In fact, in a very few short years, they may be our sole source of strength and sustenance. I believe this with my whole heart, and I am look-ing forward to its actual fulfillment. Scary? You're darn tootin' it's scary! As a man of this day and age, I am called upon to make my living by taking what is available in circumstances, and act in a common sense manner concerning my finances, needs, etc. Now God tells me to depend on Him for everything! God wants us to keep our desires, plans, and needs in His hands because, for one thing, He is very good at changing people's plans at a moment's notice. Can you think of any biblical figure who DIDN'T get their plans changed even after they became God's servants? Even today we see God sending His SINCERE WORKERS all over the place. If we say we want to live for God's glory, are you and I going to be given a special exemption? We know that God is never going to force you and me to do anything for the furtherance of His Kingdom—but how many wonderful blessings are we going to miss out on by not following Him? As far as you are concerned, the best thing you can do is hide behind me, and continue in obedience and fervent prayer. In that way YOU are not in any danger of reproach, attack or of being responsible for any actions we may take as man and wife. It is then up to me to discern that definite and sure voice of the Lord. I know that the Lord will speak to me most often through others, and most assuredly through my wife. (That's going to be you, sweetheart). I want so much for you to remain tuned in to what the Lord and I are planning. That means communication on my part and an interest on your part. Your suggestions will be and always have been welcomed, and are definitely prayed about. Would you believe that in our life together, that TWO HEADS ARE NOT BETTER THAN ONE? The Lord just now showed me that! He is THE head, and we simply obey. The last thing the Lord needs is another head or two to tell Him what His will for our lives is. Amen? By giving Him our needs and plan, we are simply acknowledging the fact that we have read, understood, and are obeying His words in MATTHEW 6. And by realizing that by giving Him our needs, we are being OBEDIENT, the needs being met have no chance of becoming the end in itself. Does that make sense? In other words, we are not giving Him all our needs just to have them met. It seems as if that is what the Jews of the Old Testament were doing. They were not grateful to the Lord for His protection and great and wonderful miracles, because their hearts were not right with God. They seemed to grudgingly cling to God, simply because they wanted to live in safety and security. Let's give our all to God out of a loving and obedient heart, ok, sweetie? OK! Jesus Christ's plan is not an option that God is offering you and me. I must tell you that we aren't free to choose anymore, simply because God has been wonderful enough to take us past the point of no return. Your sanity and health are acutely dependent on your fellowship with God in your life. Am I right? And in my life, if I was to go back and turn from the ways of the Lord, I guarantee you, I would be the most miserable, rotten, meanest and no doubt emptiest ons-fo-a-btihc on two feet!!

We are God's. He bought us with the price of His Son's blood shed on the cross. We read Scripture, we tell others about our love for our Lord, and we sing praises to His name in the assemblies of other Christians. We MUST rest in the blessed assurance that God wants to support and supply us in every aspect of our life together.

We are getting married in less than four weeks. It's June already, and before the month changes again, we will be joined as ONE for what God may grant a very long time. I am no fool, thinking it is going to be easy, loving Jesus and each other at the same time, living in this world. The world we live in doesn't like us, Diane, and neither does the Prince of this world like us; we are enemies. Before you and I were born, God set up a perfect plan for our lives. By being obedient to this plan, we can be fruitful in a dying world, peaceful in a distraught world, and overcomers in a society that is riddled with deception, wickedness, and haters of God.

Let's remember that ...

    ... LOVE NEVER FAILS

    ... LOVE COVERETH A MULTITUDE OF SINS

    ... LOVE CASTETH OUT ALL FEAR

With love, all fears, sins, and failures cannot touch us! These three things can be the biggest factors or tools that Satan will try to use to destroy our love for each other, and our love for God. Fear hath torment, sin brings separation, and failure breeds self-contempt. Believe me, Diane, we don't need any of those things in our home. But when we stay in the knowledge of God's love for us, then those three are nullified. In our relationship to each other, when one of us fails, "I LOVE YOU, HONEY"; when one of us sins, "YOU ARE FORGIVEN, I LOVE YOU"; when one of us encounters fear, "GOD HAS EVERYTHING UNDER CONTROL, I LOVE YOU." Being married, we are going to have to lean heavily on each other for love, trust, admonition, and strength. NEW WINE has a monthly section for special quotations from its readers. This month a gentleman wrote the following quote:

"SATAN IS NEVER GOING TO BOMB YOU UNLESS YOU START GETTING CLOSE TO THE STRATEGIC CENTER: JESUS CHRIST."

How true those words are! The closer we get to our Lord and Savior, the forces of Hell really turn on the heat. But then, Greater is He that is in you than he that is in the world! Praise Jesus! Just like Andraé Crouch says, "Where would I be if Jesus didn't love me; where would I be if Jesus didn't care?" Let me tell ya, sweetie, I am REAL GLAD that Jesus cares!

Gee, I've got to end this letter pretty soon and get to some Navy work that came up. I am so thankful for Jesus working in my life, and I'm so thankful that He has brought you into my life. As I was telling a buddy last night, when I have to leave you to come back up here, it really hits me again how lonely I was for a girl in my life. When I begin to wonder about what I'm getting myself into by getting married, I look at myself here right now, and remember how it was when I didn't have you to look forward to. You have made a big difference in my life as a man and as a Christian. Like the NEW WINE article said, you were designed to make me a complete and whole man as I was designed to make you a complete and total woman, as we complement one another. I LIKE THAT!

Please try to write me if you can; I really enjoy your letters too. I am still praying about coming home next weekend, but I will let you know just as soon as a decision is made. I do miss you, but I have to decide just when I must get certain things done at home, and when I must get other things squared away up here. As of yesterday, it looks like the ship may be up here in Charleston for a good party of July. That will mean finding us a place up here in the Charleston area. Clyde and I have already started looking, and it doesn't look like there will be any hassles. Let's pray that the Navy doesn't move me around too much before I get out! The more I think about it, the less I like being married and being in the Navy.

I LOVE YOU, DIANE, AND I GUESS YOU KNOW ALREADY, but I still like to remind you of that very wonderful reality. Please continue to keep me in your prayers that the Lord continues to teach me His wisdom and understanding, so that I may be able to share it with you and the rest of the Christian body.

Give my love to your family and I'll see ya soon.

With all my love,

Michael

My Precious Gift

A wife of noble character who can find? She is worth far more than rubies. Her husband has full confidence in her and lacks nothing of value. She brings him good not harm, all the days of her life. —Proverbs 30:10b–12

IN NO WAY DID I DESERVE any part of the greatest gift I received in April 1969: God's forgiveness and a passion for a life dedicated to His Gospel message. Free moneywise, but to live it out required humble surrender of two treasures in my heart: the freedom to live first for my own personal pleasure, and to live my dream of being a Roman Catholic priest. The new life and new dreams He would give could not be accomplished with me as a single man.

What He had for me required that I walk in covenant with another human. Three years later, during the first week of April, 1972, I was introduced through a letter to the second most precious gift of my life: Diane Louise Gleason. In no way did I deserve my second precious gift either.

From the first day we met at my mom's home, Diane captivated me with assets I had never experienced from or with anyone else. I will touch on three of them:

First, she exhibited a singular passion and hunger to know God and His Word. I perceived in her no appetite for the false or shallow. In 1963, she gave up television for Lent and has never gone back to it. I marveled at the sincerity and conviction in her eyes and in her tone of voice when she scorned many forms of worldly amusements, "There is nothing there that edifies my spirit or helps me learn about Jesus." She spoke as one hungering and thirsting for righteousness and peace, one who also suffered greatly from the selfish cruelty of others and from her own shameful failures.

She discovered in Whom forgiveness and peace were found and clung to Him for all she was worth. She inspired in me the desire to guide and protect her on her quest to know Jesus.

Second, through her actions, she tenderly taught me a gentleness and compassion for people, which was seriously lacking in my heart. Her kindnesses and tenderness to me melted this heart hardened by cruelties I too had suffered. Here was a lady in the truest sense of the word that lit a warm fire of devotion and stroked a healing balm of belonging into my lonely heart.

She never tried to seduce or snare me by her physical attractiveness. Diane's magnetism was a Holy Spirit glow that genuinely sought my best. Of all the people in my life, from 1972 to now, no one else's eyes and words have said, "Your heart is *safe* with me." For my first 21 years, I never felt truly a part of any individuals or groups with whom I shared life. From the moment she first spoke my name, her voice has been like the voice of an angel. Whether in adoration or rebuke, when she speaks to me, the sound of her voice goes straight into my heart like a melody. Diane made me feel like an appreciated and welcomed part of her life, and that made my heart feel *really* special. So, in appreciation and honor, I protected her, and did whatever was necessary to make her feel safe, too.

Third, God chose a unique vessel of affection and healing for my sin-ravaged, shamed, and wounded life. Just a week before I left for the minor seminary in the fall of 1968, I took a rare solo trip with my dad to his private Winter Park, Florida business office. When he left to get us some takeout lunch, I opened a storage closet door to get some paper to sketch on. In the next moments I inadvertently joined a wretched fraternity of millions of young boys who innocently discovered their father's stash of pornographic magazines.

It took only a few glossy images that afternoon to sear a seductive evil brand into my pubescent mind and body. Satan's twisted plan for sexual perversion had set up its first beachhead, and wickedness began to rip from my heart God's sacred and beautiful purposes for sex and the intimacy He designed for only two people to share for a lifetime. My religious but unregenerate heart and mind were totally unprepared for this new "gift" from Pandora (and Hugh Heffner).

From 1968 through 1971 at Marist Prep, each new class inherited stacks of smut hidden in the library, which emerged in the dorms after "lights out." Preparing for the priesthood in those years, I was informed that the solemn priestly vow of celibacy simply meant I would not be married. What activities I chose to engage in a "private sex life" was my business. No further commentary was added by the priests. I surrendered to my LORD Jesus in 1969, and from that point on my growing lust became an issue—no longer of acceptable self-pleasure and satisfaction, but of agony, frustration, and shame. The Holy Spirit daily convicted me that I was not honoring Him with my temple. He supernaturally and instantly took from me other vices, but this one He had purposed to work out of my heart in the crucible of obedience school.

From January 1972, when I reported to my first U.S. Navy warship, through "A" School in North Chicago and on to my second warship, I found myself surrounded 24/7 by explicit porn taped to virtually every permissible flat surface from desktops to heads (bathrooms), bunk frames, bulkheads, and overheads. From 1968 to 1974 there was no escape, no relief, and no one I could go to for help against the growing cancer of porno's addiction in my life. I was hooked and too ashamed to speak with anyone about it—especially my dearest friend, Diane. My Heavenly Father protected me from lusting after Diane, and I am so grateful that He superintended and kept my thoughts and affections pure towards her. That God-given purity protected us from defrauding each other.

Three days after we married in June 1975, I went back to sea for four months. I awoke one morning at sea in great terror. Father charged me to do the unthinkable in order to arrest my addiction so that it would not poison our family. He spoke as clearly to my spirit as I had ever heard. He assured me that there was HOPE for my seemingly hopeless and most besetting sin. I was to confess *all* to Diane and make myself completely and permanently accountable to her for my thought life. Back in the U.S., I obeyed in terror and meekness, humbling myself before her. I presented my sins to her and made no excuses. I vowed to submit to whatever she would determine to do together regarding strict safeguards and harsh consequences to bring us freedom.

By the power of the Holy Spirit in our marriage and through Diane's unrelenting *agapé* vigilance regarding my sin, we together conquered and removed that monstrous evil from us. My wife remains my faithfully alert sentry and shields me against the wiles of Satan in the protection of our holy relationship. Perhaps there is in Diane and me a future book to write for couples to help them conquer this affliction menacing their bond as well.

There is no one I would rather go into ministry around the globe with than Diane Louise Meagher. Since 1972, I have heard from far too many people who pretend to know her tell me what Diane cannot do and why. The reasons given why she should not be an independent pioneer missionary to the infamous "Black Hole" are always the same. Those who express Diane's inability to live a lifelong God adventure merely project their own fears and worldly affections through offense onto her. They discount the power and presence of God's Holy Spirit in Diane's life, given to serve Him: 2 Chronicles 16:9.[41]

Diane is the strongest and smartest woman I have ever met, and I am in awe of what she has become and accomplished for the Kingdom. Talk to anyone across the nation of Russia who has worked with her and ask them where Diane's heart and gifts lie. My precious wife is deeply loved and respected across Russia. She is still spoken about in villages across the Black Hole.

In the four decades I have walked with her, I have not seen such love and devotion for Christ in any other. I was down for the count a number of times in Siberia when the rigors and challenges to my work overwhelmed me, and Diane was there to lift

---

41. *For the eyes of the Lord run to and fro throughout the whole earth, to show Himself strong on behalf of those whose heart is loyal to Him.*

me up. Through all that she has suffered in her life in the Refiner's Fires, she still has only two desires: to love her Master and to have the opportunity to lead others to Him wherever He leads.

Wherever Diane speaks at women's groups across America, she ends with Q&A sessions. Inevitably the question is asked, "Why did you follow Mike to Siberia?" She always answers joyfully from her heart, "I didn't follow *Mike* there, I followed *Jesus* to Siberia because *I* was called there, too!"

In American professional sports, its heroes and superheroes are only eligible to be inducted into the Hall of Fame after they retire and are long ineligible to play again. We still have much more life and ministry ahead, and I have already placed her in seven categories in my Hall of Fame: extraordinary Christian, lover, mom, grandmom, musician, teacher, and missionary. It has taken all of the last 41 years to appreciate the value of the second most precious gift from my loving Father's hand.

In so many different ways for the last four decades I have been her student. She has taught me so much about love as God intended it to be. One of my favorite pastimes is to sit across from her at restaurants around the globe and just stare into her eyes. I love to open doors for her in all our travels, hold her hand wherever we walk, and for long periods at a time just gently stroke her hair. It was not good that Mike Meagher be alone. And thank God he isn't.

Five Foundational Prayers

O UR GOD HAS A ZEAL for His house to be a place where nothing unclean or unholy enters. Wherever He placed His glory, He required sentries to guard what is holy, beginning with fiery angels at the gates of Eden. Within the first four years of my walk with my Father, He set these sentries of truth and wisdom to guard this fleshly tabernacle of His presence.

I have kept these five prayers/contemplations close by my bed since my Navy days, and each in an appropriate moment reminds me of what is of *most* value as I choose how to invest my trials, contemplations, time, energy, and resources.

Five prayers: Scriptures I personalized and go back to in testing my daily allegiance to them:

1. Based on 2 Timothy 2:3–4[42]: *"LORD, as I follow You, I am going to see what others have that this world offers, and I am going to really want many of those things that have value and bring comfort now by the world's standards. PLEASE do not give me what would—if I had it—rob me of the eternal fruit for which You put me here."*

2. Based on 1 Corinthians 6:19–20[43]: *"Father, I know that my body is a temple of Your Holy Spirit, who is in me, whom I have received from You. I am not my own; I was bought at the price of*

---

42. *You therefore must endure hardship as a good soldier of Jesus Christ. No one engaged in warfare entangles himself with the affairs of this life, that he may please him who enlisted him as a soldier.*

43. *Or do you not know that your body is the temple of the Holy Spirit who is in you, whom you have from God, and you are not your own? For you were bought at a price; therefore glorify God in your body and in your spirit, which are God's.*

Your Son's precious blood. Therefore, I desire to honor You in and with this body."

3. Based on Isaiah 61:1–3[44] and Luke 4:18–19[45]: *"Father, You placed your Sovereign Spirit on me, because You anointed me to proclaim Good News to the poor, to bind up the brokenhearted, to proclaim freedom for the captives and release from darkness for the prisoners. To proclaim Your favor and to warn of the coming day of Your vengeance, to comfort all who mourn, and provide for those who grieve to bestow on them a crown of beauty instead of ashes, the oil of joy instead of mourning, and a garment of praise instead of a spirit of despair. So please give me a divine appointment today, Father, that I might be Your conduit of this grace."*

4. Based on my life verse, 1 John 3:16[46]: *"Father, Your Son laid down His life for me, and now I am yours, and You have filled me*

---

44. *"The Spirit of the Lord God is upon Me,*
Because the Lord has anointed Me
To preach good tidings to the poor;
He has sent Me to heal the brokenhearted,
To proclaim liberty to the captives,
And the opening of the prison to those who are bound;
To proclaim the acceptable year of the Lord,
And the day of vengeance of our God;
To comfort all who mourn,
To console those who mourn in Zion,
To give them beauty for ashes,
The oil of joy for mourning,
The garment of praise for the spirit of heaviness;
That they may be called trees of righteousness,
The planting of the Lord, that He may be glorified."

45. *"The Spirit of the Lord is upon Me,*
Because He has anointed Me
To preach the gospel to the poor;
He has sent Me to heal the brokenhearted,
To proclaim liberty to the captives
And recovery of sight to the blind,
To set at liberty those who are oppressed;
To proclaim the acceptable year of the Lord."

46. *By this we know love, because He laid down His life for us. And we also ought to lay down our lives for the brethren.*

with Your Spirit, so direct my steps and show me today someone whom You would be pleased for me to lay down my life and priorities for, that he or she might come to know You."

5. Based on Daniel 12:1–3[47]: "*Father, I trust what You told Your servant Daniel that there will be a time of distress such as has not happened from the beginning of nations but at that time your people—everyone whose name is found written in the book—will be delivered. THANK YOU! Multitudes who sleep in the dust of the earth will awake, some to everlasting life, others to shame and everlasting contempt. You said that those who are wise will shine like the brightness of the heavens, and those who lead many to righteousness, like the stars for ever and ever. Father, please give me precious souls who might be granted everlasting life and be delivered from eternal shame and contempt.*"

---

47. "*At that time Michael shall stand up,*
The great prince who stands watch over the sons of your people;
And there shall be a time of trouble,
Such as never was since there was a nation,
Even to that time.
And at that time your people shall be delivered,
Every one who is found written in the book.
And many of those who sleep in the dust of the earth shall awake,
Some to everlasting life,
Some to shame and everlasting contempt.
Those who are wise shall shine
Like the brightness of the firmament,
And those who turn many to righteousness
Like the stars forever and ever.

Six Foundational Attitudes

THESE SIX QUOTES ARE A part of me and stay at the forefront of my mind in the toughest of times. What gives them most weight in my heart is that those who spoke or wrote them *lived* them. They lived lives I want to emulate. When the Holy Spirit put one on my heart directly, He did so that I might live it by His power. Those I received from others, I give their names:

1. American missionary and martyr Jim Elliott: *"He is no fool who gives up what he cannot keep to gain that which he cannot lose."*

2. 19th century evangelist and humble shoe salesman, Dwight L. Moody: *"If we are full of pride and conceit and ambition and self-seeking and pleasure and the world, there is no room for the Spirit of God, and I believe many a man is praying to God to fill him when he is full already with something else."*

3. The British Isles evangelist Mr. Henry Varley inspired D. L. Moody with this statement: *"The world has yet to see what God will do with and for and through and in and by the man who is fully consecrated to Him."*

4. My personal ponytailed hero and pioneer missionary to Native Americans David Brainerd wrote in the 1700s: *"We should always look upon ourselves as God's servants, placed in God's world, to do his work; and accordingly labour faithfully for him; not with a design to grow rich and great, but to glorify God, and do all the good we possibly can."*

5. The Holy Spirit spoke to my heart: *"The safest place on this planet is in the center of My will. Trust Me!"*

6. *"I am not afraid of failure. I am afraid of succeeding at the wrong things."* —William Carey

Spending Time with God

GOD SENT US HIS POWER, glory, and presence in Jesus Christ, who on a cruel Roman cross took in His body the punishment for our sin and rebellion. Today, we who are His know His eternal forgiveness and access to His throne of grace. For the God of the universe does not dwell in religious buildings or in icons made by men. He dwells in His heavenly throne room and in the hearts of true believers daily changed by His Spirit:

Do you not know that your body is the temple of the Holy Spirit within you, which you have from God? —1 Corinthians 6:19

When God cleansed us and filled us with His Holy Spirit, we entered into a unique relationship of intimacy and love with the Creator and Sustainer of the universe.

At our new birth, He began a process of changing and conforming us into the likeness of Jesus Christ to reflect the light, and love of His nature in a world of darkness and hatred. Fear is replaced by trust and faith through prayer. Daily freedom from our old master, Satan, and sin, come through the intimate power and presence of God's Holy Spirit.

This special and unique relationship between us and our Heavenly Father requires quality time and two-way communication. He invites us to be still and become aware of His presence and love. He longs to provide every need if we will daily quiet our soul and come away daily for intimate fellowship with Him.

Prayer satisfies hunger. It satisfies God's vast hunger for a relationship with us, and our insatiable hunger for God. *God wants to speak to us more than we want to listen.* God is love, and love longs to communicate. If we do not wait patiently in expectation of God in prayer, our minds lose the discipline of discernment between what leads us closer to God and what doesn't, and our hearts lose their spiritual sensitivity.

The Lord is my shepherd, I shall not want; He makes me lie down in green pastures. He leads me beside still waters; He restores my soul. —Psalm 23:1–3

Prayer is being alone with our omnipotent loving God. Like eating and drinking for the natural body, prayer fills the deepest hunger of our soul and spirit. Prayer, however practiced, is hunger for God satisfied by His loving presence. How does that hunger express itself in our lives? God invites us to the inner banquet of life.

It is Jesus who moves us to approach our Father by the Holy Spirit as He "knocks" on our hearts (Revelation 3:20), making known His desire to enter and to give us strength, encouragement, cleansing, and blessed daily hope through precious fellowship with the Holy Trinity. We are made in the image of God to worship and enjoy Him now and for eternity. In His light is true life.

Perhaps we are unwilling to pray daily because we are trapped by sinful habits we will not abandon, and our guilt overwhelms and shames us into fleeing from Him in our hearts. Whatever the reason for our lack of intimacy with God, there is good news. He waits to embrace us in His arms of unconditional forgiveness and love. Communion with God is very difficult when we hold things back, and are not genuine with Him or ourselves about our rebellion in habitual sins:

If I had cherished sin in my heart, the Lord would not have listened. —Psalm 66:18 (NIV)

Perhaps we cleave to vain pleasures, evil thoughts, or attitudes such as unforgiveness that rob us of our joy and eternal fruit, afraid that we must surrender them in repentance. It is here we are challenged in the truth that we love our sin more than we love Him. We thus forsake the fountain of living waters for broken cisterns that cannot satisfy (Jeremiah 2:13), keeping us from our God Who alone can heal, cleanse, and fully satisfy.

He wants to free us from our chains, but without daily prayer it is easy to grow deaf to His voice of divine love and become spiritually deaf and confused by the many opposing voices that demand our attention—and want us to serve them. God's words bring healing and life.

Have we blocked His entrance into any hidden room of our hearts? What or who is in those rooms? Jesus is asking for access to *all* of our heart—our needs and desires. Jesus is knocking on those doors. What is our response? What in our heart today makes Him sad?

Often, when we try to pray, troubling thoughts from the world, our flesh, and evil spirits try to distract us. Such thoughts can be deafening. When troubled with worldly thoughts, what is holy becomes distant. Yet, His soft voice calls us apart to rest and peace. This prayer journal is offered to help focus on the Holy One.

I have given you my prayer journal as a gift and tool to help you meditate and focus on the character and nature of God, His past, present, and future path into His glorious love and image, and to help you in prayer to discover who you are in Him. Come with me and find rest, comfort, strength, and joy in His presence:

You will make known to me the path of life; in Your presence is fullness of joy; in Your right hand there is pleasure forever. —Psalm 16:16

The more time we spend in our Father's presence, the more in the likeness of His Son we become.

Your servant and His,
Pastor Michael Meagher
June, 1987

My Daily Prayer Journal

*I*T IS VITAL THAT *I spend time alone, undisturbed, and undistracted, SPEAK praise aloud to my Heavenly Father. Between each of the four sections, I must take precious time for silence to hear from Him.*

1. ADORATION

GOD MY FATHER, You are ...	
Creator of All	All Wise
The Most High One	Lord of All
Infinite in Power	Hateful of Sin
Infinite in Love	Pure Light
Infinite in Glory	Full of Mercy
Infinitely Perfect	Incorruptible
All Knowledge	All Sufficient
Infinite in Beauty	Perfect in Unity
Infinite Peace	Slow to Anger
Holy in Purpose	Compassionate
Perfect Goodness	At Perfect Rest
The Holy One	Without Fear
Unchanging	Infinitely Kind
All Pure	Always Present
All Truth	Worthy of Praise
Infinite	Worthy of Honor

JESUS MY SAVIOR, You ...	
are all that the Father is.	are my Advocate.
sacrificed Your life.	are my Lord.
took my shame.	are my First Love.
bore my iniquity.	are my Savior.
reconciled me.	are my King.
reward obedience.	are my Redeemer.
will never leave me.	are my Master.
will never forsake me.	are Righteous Judge.
was tempted as I am.	reward iniquity.
are my way of escape.	are coming soon.
are Giver of life eternal.	are without sin.

HOLY SPIRIT MY COMFORTER, You . . .	
indwell me.	pray through me.
teach me.	are my Divine Helper.
guide me.	strengthen me.
warn me.	search me.
comfort me.	seal me.
sustain me.	give me hope.
convict me.	lift me up.
quicken me.	give me faith.
are my Interpreter.	embolden me.
are my Power Source.	

As one, Your Spirit and Word bring pure fruit in my life, and separate my soul and spirit, the thoughts and intents of my heart.

2. CONTRITION

MY SINS OF OMISSION	
Lack of faith	Lack of prayer
Lack of peace	Lack of trust
Lack of faithfulness	Lack of love
Lack of obedience	Lack of purity

MY SINS OF COMMISSION	
Unbelief	Lusts of the eyes
Selfishness	Lusts of the flesh
Pride	Unforgiveness
Anger	Ungodly thoughts
The world's friendship	Wasting time
Vain imaginations	Other specific sins

3. THANKSGIVING

YOUR BLESSINGS PAST	
My origins	My salvation
My family	Past victories
Your love	My talents
Your calling	Forgiveness
Your gifts	My design
Your healings	My training

YOUR BLESSINGS PRESENT	
Perseverance	Your Word
Joy	Your presence
Peace	Your protection
My family	Your tools
Your ministry	Special gifts
Present victories	Your provision
My friends	Other blessings

YOUR BLESSINGS FUTURE
For victory in our work
For the church universal
Free from evil's presence
Rewards of the righteous
My new body and home
Righteous judgment on evil
Eternity in Your presence

4. SUPPLICATION

YOUR KINGDOM'S NEEDS	OTHERS' NEEDS
Your will done in Your people	Your people walking in obedience
Your glory revealed	Your people thriving in prayer
Your power manifested	Be revealed to Your people
Workers into the harvest	Deliverance from evil
Word of Satan destroyed	For parents, kids, and grandkids
Culmination of all things	Specific needs & requests of others

MY NEEDS	
My holiness unto You, Lord	My health and strength for Your work
My humility for Your work	My focus for Your work
My wisdom for Your work	My specific needs and requests

Are You Ready?

A S SMALL CHILDREN WE LEARN to be ready for each day's assigned tasks. For every duty, we prepare. If we were not ready when we arrived at the time and place of duty, we were shamed and not accepted. When momma called, "Let's eat!" we had a *conditional* right to the family table. It was an invitation and a warning. It was an *invitation* to enjoy food, friends, and fellowship. It was also a *warning*—a *condition*—to come appropriately ready. We learned that, when we were called, we were to stop and consider if we were ready to eat. If we went to the family table naked, with dirty hands, drunk, or "stuffed" from unhealthy junk food like candy, we dishonored our family and guests, were turned away, and were shamed in front of all.

Imagine the ultimate dream: to be invited to a great celestial banquet. Imagine your joy and honor when personally invited to attend an exquisite feast given by a greatly esteemed world leader of great wealth. At this feast, every delectable food is served. All the fresh fruits, vegetables, meats, breads, and desserts closest to your heart are served with the world's finest beverages. The feast is served for many, many days, and you are never filled. Eat all you wish. At this banquet are the world's greatest people of history who consider you their equal. You arrive and are announced with honor and given personal escort to your place at the table by the famous host. You speak to all from your heart.

There is a catch: THIS FEAST IS REAL and is coming *soon*. You have this life only to get ready, so how will you equip yourself? What will you wear? How will you plan so as not to embarrass yourself? What will it be like if you arrive at this magnificent formal feast naked, dirty, drunk, not hungry, and unprepared to speak? How deep will be your shame before the eyes of *all*?

Truly as I live, as a servant and ordained messenger of the living God, I officially declare to you, my reader, that on behalf of the Lord of the universe, you're now reading a personal invitation to His formal banquet.

Bible prophecy declares that at this very moment He is making preparations for the greatest feast in history. I solemnly challenge you that Jesus Christ will return with great power and glory. At the moment of His arrival, He will destroy all evil and punish all who practice evil by great plagues and eternal fire. When He has purged this planet, as gold and silver are made pure in a furnace, He will begin His global eternal Kingdom. The inauguration of His new world and Kingdom will begin with a banquet as described in the above "dream." Today, God is among all peoples, *inviting* all to come. God warns today: get ready for His banquet or be eternally shamed. You have four problems that will keep you out. He wants you to sit at His table and not shamed and rejected before the whole world.

1. You are naked: Jesus Christ spoke many things, which are written in the Bible, about His second coming to earth in power to conquer this world and destroy all evil. He warns you now to be wearing the white robe of His holiness so that you might walk with Him in peace and not be ashamed:

*"You say, `I am rich, with all I want; I don't need a thing!' And you don't realize that spiritually you are wretched and miserable and poor and blind and NAKED. —*Revelation 3:17

*"Beware: I will come as suddenly as a thief! Blessed are all who are awaiting me, who keep their robes in ready and will not need to walk NAKED and ashamed." —*Revelation 16:15

Because of our sin and rebellion against God, we are open, shamed, and naked before His eyes. We are clothed in front of the eyes of one another—but God sees into our hearts and souls. God is pure and holy, and all who walk in His presence must walk in a pure white robe given only by Jesus Christ. Only those wearing the pure robes of the righteousness of Jesus worn on the banquet day will be accepted.

2. You have dirty hands: Since your youth, you have used your mind, your feet, and especially your hands to do evil against God. If you did evil only once, you have added to the evil of this world that God will destroy. No one with dirty hands will eat at His table. Only Jesus Christ can totally clean them.

Wash your hands, you sinners, and let your hearts be filled with God alone to make them pure and true to him. Let there be tears for the wrong things you have done. —James 4:8–9

3. You are drunk: Those who are sober can see trouble coming and react to it with wisdom. But those who are drunk are blind to trouble and are unable to prepare for safety. You are drunk with sin and the pleasures of this world that blind you to eternity and your need to prepare for it. Jesus compared our world in this day of His return to the ancient wicked city of Babylon. He said in His destruction of evil:

"Babylon the Great is fallen; she has become a den of demons, a haunt of devils and every kind of evil spirit. For all the nations have drunk the fatal wine of her intense immorality. The rulers of earth have enjoyed themselves with her, and businessmen throughout the world have grown rich from all her luxurious living." —Revelation 18:2–3

4. You are not hungry: You wake up every morning and go to bed in the evening hungry for physical food and hungry for the things this temporary evil world can give you. You hunger for that which will satisfy the lusts of your eyes (all that looks good), the lusts of your flesh (all that feels good), and the pride of life (all that will make you feel important). These you eat like bread without regard to good and evil. You have no desire to eat all the special and good things God has for you. You are not hungry and thirsty for God and His goodness and friendship in your life. Jesus said:

"Blessed are those who hunger and thirst for righteousness, for they shall be satisfied. —Matthew 5:5–6

Do not work for food that spoils, but for food that endures to eternal life, which I will give you. On him God the Father has placed his seal of approval." —John 6:27

Almost 2,000 years ago, God's only Son Jesus Christ was nailed to a cruel Roman cross for one purpose. God looked down through time and saw your rebellion and sin. He saw your nakedness, dirty hands and heart, your hunger and thirst for evil. He knew every evil thought and action. He knew that you would never be able to clean yourself or change yourself to be perfect enough to enjoy His presence and love forever. So God sent His perfect, clean, and holy Son Jesus from Heaven to be punished and killed to pay the full and perfect price for your freedom from Satan's kingdom, and to give you His clean and spotless white robe for the great banquet coming soon:

Jesus said, "Be prepared—all dressed and ready—for your Lord's return from the wedding feast. Then you will be ready to open the door and let Him in the moment He arrives and knocks. There will be great joy for those who are ready and waiting for His return. He Himself will seat them and put on a waiter's uniform and serve them as they sit and eat! He may come at nine o'clock at night—or even at midnight. But whenever He comes, there will be joy for His servants who are ready!"
—Luke 12:35–38

Jesus said to them, "I am the bread of life; he who comes to Me will not hunger, and he who believes in Me will never thirst. But I said to you that you have seen Me, and yet do not believe. All that the Father gives Me will come to Me, and the one who comes to Me I will certainly not cast out. For I have come down from heaven, not to do My own will, but the will of Him who sent Me. This is the will of Him who sent Me, that of all that He has given Me I lose nothing, but raise it up on the last day. For this is the will of My Father, that everyone who beholds the Son and believes in Him will have eternal life, and I Myself will raise him up on the last day." —John 6:35–40

I assure you that very, very soon this world will enter a period of terrible suffering, war, famine, and unequaled hatred of men for one another. Satan will present a world leader to try to destroy all good and those who do good in God's name. It is Satan's and his demons' last attempt to get man's worship and bring souls with them into eternal fire. This terrible time will test the heart and soul of every man and woman. At the appointed moment, Jesus Christ will appear, draw all believers to Himself in safety, and cleanse this planet of every evil, eternally condemning all evil spirits to eternal chains and fire. All those who chose to remain spiritually naked, dirty, drunk, and full with the desires of this world, chose to be eternally shamed, with Satan and his demons in chains and fire. Whom will you join for eternity? How will you get ready? Here is God's simple plan and free gifts to you—a spotless white robe, clean hands, His forgiveness, and a pure heart:

Right now with your heart and mouth, agree with God that you have disobeyed him and lived in rebellion to His love.

For if you tell others with your own mouth that Jesus Christ is your Lord and believe in your own heart that God has raised Him from the dead, you will be saved. For it is by believing in his heart that a man becomes right with God; and with his mouth he tells others of his faith, confirming his salvation. —Romans 10:9–10

Agree with Him that His Son Jesus Christ, died on a cross to pay for all your sin, and that you accept His payment for your sin.

And just as it is destined that men die only once, and after that comes judgment, so also Christ died only once as an offering for the sins of many people; and He will come again, but not to deal again with our sins. This time He will come bringing salvation to all those who are eagerly and patiently waiting for Him. —Hebrews 9:27–28

Ask God to free you from all bondage to Satan and his evil kingdom that have kept you bound to sin and shame.

For He has rescued us out of the darkness and gloom of Satan's kingdom and brought us into the Kingdom of His dear Son, who bought our freedom with His blood and forgave us all our sins. —Colossians 1:13–14

4. Ask God to clean your heart and to turn your eyes and heart from this world to love and serve Him.

And so I would say to you who are suffering, God will give you rest along with us when the Lord Jesus appears suddenly from heaven in flaming fire with His mighty angels, bringing judgment on those who do not wish to know God and who refuse to accept His plan to save them through our Lord Jesus Christ. They will be punished in everlasting hell, forever separated from the Lord, never to see the glory of His power when He comes to receive praise and admiration because of all He has done for His people, His saints. And you will be among those praising Him because you have believed what we told you about Him. —2 Thessalonians 1:7–10

5. Ask Him to fill you with His Holy Spirit and power to live for Him and be happy to see Him when He comes.

We wait for the blessed hope—the glorious appearing of our great God and Savior, Jesus Christ, who gave Himself for us to redeem us from all wickedness and to purify for Himself a people that are His very own, eager to do what is good. —Titus 2:13–14

If you have called out to God from your heart, and asked Him through His Son Jesus Christ to clean, forgive, and give you eternal life, God promises you that you will be wearing a white robe on the soon day of Jesus' return, and you will sit at the great banquet table of God with all the rescued of human history. Rejoice, and walk with God in the freedom of purity each day, that you might reflect His purity and tell others of the love He is placing in your heart. In obedience to His commands, be baptized as a symbol and statement to the world that you no longer belong to it, and join with other believers in the communion of bread and wine:

For I received from the Lord what I also delivered to you, that the Lord Jesus on the night when He was betrayed took bread, and when He had given thanks, He broke it, and said, "This is My body which is for you. Do this in remembrance of Me." In the same way also the cup, after supper, saying, "This cup is the new covenant in My blood. Do this, as often as you drink it, in remembrance of Me. For as often as you eat this bread and drink the cup, you proclaim the Lord's death until He comes. —1 Corinthians 11:23–26

In and through the love of Jesus Christ,
Pastor Michael Meagher
1987